CAVENDISH LAWCards®

Succession

Cavendish
Publishing
Limited

First published in Great Britain 1997 by Cavendish Publishing Limited, The Glass House, Wharton Street, London WC1X 9PX.

Telephone: 0171-278 8000 Facsimile: 0171-278 8080

Lawcard on succession

1.Inheritance and succession - England 2.Inheritance and succession - England - Examinations, questions, etc.

I.Succession

344.2'0652

ISBN 1 85941 325 0

Printed and bound in Great Britain

Contents

1 The general nature of wills

Introduction

What is a will?

A will has been judicially defined as 'the aggregate of [a man's] testamentary intentions, so far as they are manifested in writing, duly executed according to statute' – *per* Sir JP Wilde in *Lemage v Goodban* (1865).

An equally instructive definition is found in *Jarman on Wills*. Jarman's definition which has been endorsed in *Re Berger* (1989) and *Baird v Baird* (1990) states that a will is 'an instrument by which a person makes a disposition of his property to take effect after his decease and which is in its own nature ambulatory and revocable during his lifetime'.

Characteristics of a will

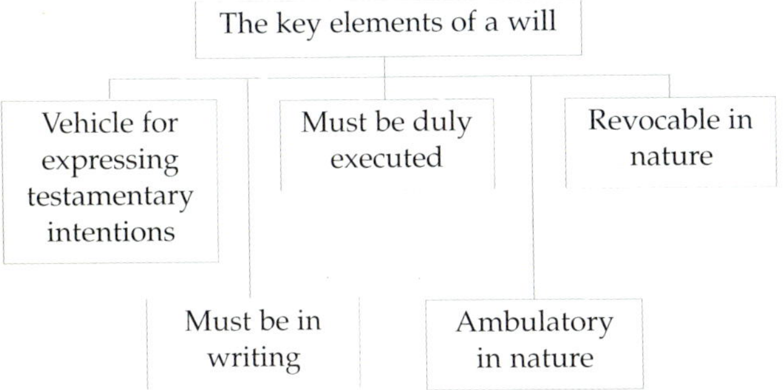

Using the above two definitions as our point of reference, it is possible to elaborate on the main characteristics of wills.

(a) The definition in *Lemage* refers to 'testamentary intentions'. The primary purpose of a will is to enable a person to give directions regarding the manner in which his affairs are to be conducted after his death. Such a person is called a testator, if male, or testatrix, if female (both of which shall be denoted by the letter T). The contents of a will represent T's testamentary intentions and provided T is of sound mind and has attained majority, English law gives effect to such intentions when T dies.

(b) As seen from Jarman's definition, the intentions expressed by T in his will are usually concerned with 'the disposition of his property ... after his decease'. Very often, however, the directions contained in a will cover other matters such as:

- the appointment, functions and remuneration of executors;
- the appointment of guardians for T's infant children;
- payment of taxes, death duties and T's debts;
- funeral arrangements and other issues relating to the disposal of T's body.

(c) The reference to writing in *Lemage* as well as Jarman's description of a will as an *instrument* reflect the fact that in English law a will is not ordinarily enforceable unless T expresses his wishes in documentary form.

These wishes are usually embodied in one document but it is not uncommon for T to employ two or more documents (for instance, where he amends an aspect of his will by means of a supplementary document known as a *codicil*). Where he does so, 'it is the aggregate or the net result that constitutes his will' (see *Douglas-Menzies v Umphelby* (1908)).

(d) It emerges from *Lemage* that a will has to be *'duly executed according to statute'*. The statutory provisions governing the execution of a will are dealt with in the next chapter.

(e) As Jarman's definition indicates, a will is *ambulatory*. This means that it does not take effect in T's lifetime but only on his death (see *Countess of Berkeley v Berkeley* (1946); *Re Batty* (1952); *Re Cairnes* (1982); *Re Berger* and *Miller v Callender* (1993)). This has far-reaching implications. In particular:

- While T is alive, the contents of his will are mere declarations of intention which do not bind him. For example, if T devises Blackacre to B in his will, he can still sell it at a later date.
- A beneficiary under a will acquires no interest until T's death so that if he dies before T, the gift ordinarily lapses.
- Property belonging to T at his death is capable of devolving under his will, even if it had not yet been acquired at the time the will was executed. For example, if T makes a will, devising 'all my real property to B' and T later buys a house, which he retains till his death, the house will pass to B under the will.

(f) Jarman's definition also states that a will is *revocable* in T's lifetime. T's capacity to revoke is so fundamental that it is not lost even where he declares in his will that it is irrevocable (see *Vynior's case* (1609)); or enters into an agreement not to revoke it (see *Robinson v Omanney* (1882)).

Special types of wills

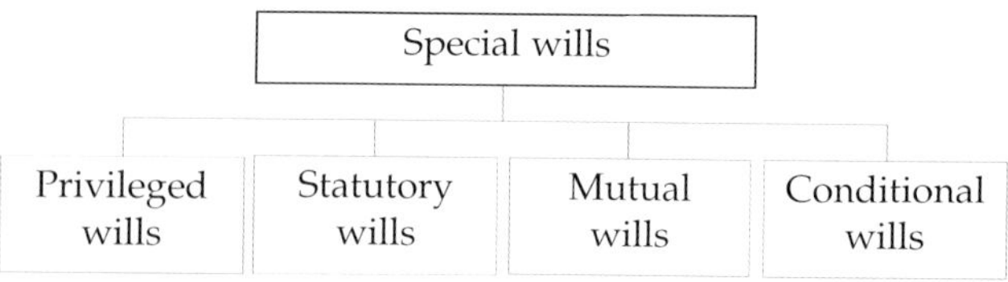

Thus far, we have concentrated on the attributes of conventional wills. There are, however, various categories of wills which differ from conventional wills in significant respects. These include:

Privileged wills

As seen above, a conventional will must be in writing and duly executed. This requirement is, however, dispensed with in the case of privileged wills, which are wills made by members of the armed forces while in actual military service or by seamen while at sea. The nature of privileged wills and the conditions for their validity are dealt with in the next chapter.

Statutory wills

It was also mentioned above that a will can only take effect if T is of sound mind when executing it. It follows that a mental patient cannot ordinarily make a will. The Court of Protection is, however, empowered by s 96(e) Mental Health Act 1983 to order a statutory will to be executed by an authorised person on behalf of an adult mental patient.

A statutory will must comply with the requirements in s 97 MHA, as follows:

- it must be expressed to be signed by the patient, acting through the authorised person;
- it must be signed by the authorised person in the patient's name and with his own name in the joint presence of two witnesses who must also sign it in the presence of the authorised person;
- it must bear the official seal of the Court of Protection.

Cases in which effect has been given to statutory wills include:

Case	Description of patient
Re Davey (1981):	92 year old nursing home resident who had become incapable of managing her own affairs.
Re D(J) (1982):	Elderly widow who had gone to live with her daughter when she could no longer take care of herself.
Re C (A Patient) (1991):	75 year old psychiatric patient who had been mentally ill since birth.

Mutual wills

These are wills made by two persons on the basis of an agreement between them that when they each die, their estates shall devolve in a specified manner.

Mutual wills are commonly framed in identical or similar terms, with each party leaving their property in the first instance to the other and thereafter to the same person(s).

Such wills are most often used by spouses in order to ensure that when they both die their property shall pass to the same persons (usually their issue). The wills may provide:

- that property belonging to each spouse shall pass to the other *for life*, remainder to their issue (or other beneficiaries) (ee *Gray v Perpetual Trustee Co Ltd* (1928) and *Re Hagger* (1930));
- that property belonging to each spouse shall pass to the other spouse *absolutely* with a *substitutionary provision* to the effect that if the other spouse dies first, the property shall devolve on their issue (see *Re Cleaver* (1981));
- that when each spouse dies, his/her property will pass to the issue with no provision for the other spouse (see *Re Dale* (1993)).

It is with regard to revocation that mutual wills differ materially from ordinary wills. The position in this regard may be summarised as follows:

Ordinary wills:	Revocable throughout T's lifetime.
Mutual wills:	Where both parties are still alive: Either may revoke (although the other may seek damages for breach of contract). *Dufour v Pereira* (1769); *Stone v Hoskins* (1905).
	After the death of one party: • **At law**: Survivor is free to revoke his will. • **In equity**: Freedom to revoke is curtailed by imposing constructive trust on survivor's estate. See *Dufour v Pereira*; *Re Hagger*; *Re Cleaver*; *Re Dale*. *Note*: The constructive trust will be imposed only if there is evidence that both parties agreed not to revoke their respective wills (see *Goodchild v Goodchild* (1995)).

Conditional wills

Absolute wills: take effect immediately on T's death

Wills which appear at first sight to be conditional but which are construed as ordinary wills

Conditional wills: take effect on T's death only if prescribed event occurs

A noteable characteristic of an ordinary will is that it comes into effect as soon as T dies. It is, however, open to T to stipulate that his will shall be conditional upon the occurrence or fulfilment of a stated event or requirement. As seen from cases such as *In the Goods of Robinson* (1870); *Lindsay v Lindsay* (1872) and *Re Thomas* (1939) such a conditional will does not take effect on T's death unless the prescribed condition has been satisfied.

It is not, however, that it is not in every case where a will discloses that T had a particular event in mind when making it, that the will is conditional on the occurrence of that event. See, eg:

- *In the Goods of Cawthorn* (1863), where the wording of the will suggested that it was meant to take effect only if T did not return from a long journey on which he was about to embark. There was, however, evidence that T executed the will after making the journey and the court deduced from this that he did not intend the will to be conditional on his non-return.
- *In the Goods of Dobson* (1866) and *Re Vines* (1910) which held that the future events referred to in the respective wills were not meant to be conditions but merely served to explain why the wills were made.

The courts have recently found it necessary to determine whether extrinsic evidence can be relied on to prove that T intended his will to be conditional, where the material condition is not referred to in the will itself. In *Corbett v Newey* (1994), the trial court concluded that such evidence was admissible but a year later it was decided on appeal that for there to be a conditional will, the condition must appear on the face of the will.

Contracts pertaining to wills

Contract to make a will

Where T enters into an agreement with B, to make a will leaving property to B, there is a valid contract, provided the agreement:

- is under seal or supported by consideration;
- is intended to create legal relations (see *McPhail v Torrance* (1909) and *Parker v Clark* (1960)); and
- is in writing as required by s 2 Law of Property (Miscellaneous Provisions) Act 1989, where the property is land.

T may be in breach of the contract in the following situations:

- Where T decides not to make the will: B cannot compel T to make the will, but on T's death, may recover the property from T's personal representatives or claim damages out of his estate.
- Where T makes a will but does not in fact leave the property to B as agreed: B cannot compel T to revoke the will but may again be entitled to the property or damages in lieu thereof (see *Hammersley v De Biel* (1845)).

- Where T makes a will leaving the property to B but then decides to revoke the will: B cannot compel T not to revoke but may be entitled to damages in the event of such revocation.

Note, however, if the will is revoked by T's subsequent marriage, this does not amount to a breach (see *Re Marsland* (1939)).

- Where T proceeds to dispose of the property in his lifetime: B may claim damages against T. B may also have a good title to the property against the recipient unless the latter was a *bona fide* purchaser for value without notice (see *Synge v Synge* (1894)). Moreover, if B has prior knowledge of T's plan to dispose of the property, B may obtain a declaration of right and an injunction against T (see *Schaeffer v Schumann* (1972)).

Note, however, that if T contracts to leave his entire estate or a specified share of his estate to B, this refers to whatever is left at T's death. Accordingly, there will be no breach if T disposes of his entire estate in his lifetime.

Contract not to revoke a will

Where T, having made a will leaving property to B, enters into an agreement with B not to revoke the will, this may also constitute a valid contract.

B cannot obtain an injunction to restrain T from revoking the will (but note the position with regard to mutual wills at p 6 above). If T does revoke, however, B may recover damages from T (or his personal representatives if he has died) except in the case of revocation by marriage (see *Robinson v Omanney* (1882)).

Alternative methods of disposing of property on death

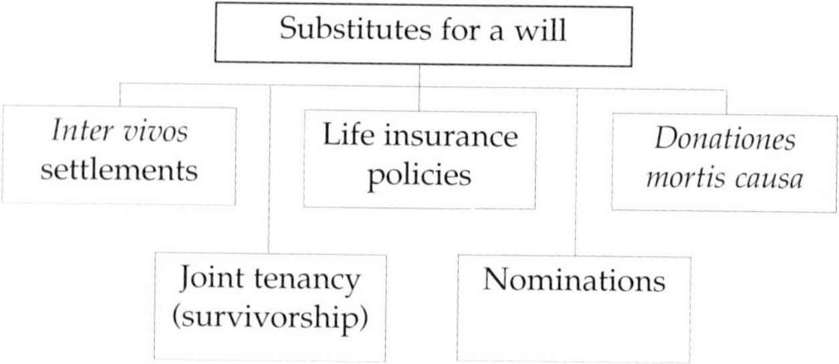

A will is not the only method of disposing of property on death. Other methods include the following:

Inter vivos dispositions

Inter vivos dispositions differ from wills in two respects:

- The formal requirements which must be observed in making a will are not the same as those for *inter vivos* transfers;
- A will ordinarily comes into effect on T's death, while an *inter vivos* disposition takes effect once it is made or on the occurrence of an event other than the maker's death.

Some scope does however exist for a property owner who wants to enjoy his property in his lifetime and leave it to another person on his death to realise his objective by making an *inter vivos* disposition rather than a will. For example, if O, the owner of Blackacre, wishes to pass it to B after his death, O may execute a deed *inter vivos* in which he conveys Blackacre to T on trust for O for life, remainder to B while at the same time reserving for himself (ie O) a power to revoke the gift to B.

Survivorship under joint tenancies

Where A and B resolve that whichever one of them dies first, his property will pass to the survivor, the usual course is for them to execute separate wills or a joint will to this effect.

A similar result may, however, be achieved where A and B arrange for the property concerned to be held by them as joint tenants. If either party then dies without the joint tenancy having been severed, the property automatically devolves on the other one by virtue of the right of survivorship (*jus accrescendi*).

Benefits payable under life insurance policy

A person who wishes to provide for others after his death, may also do so by means of an insurance policy on his life. Under such a policy, the insurer in return for premiums paid by the policyholder (ie the person taking out the policy) undertakes to pay an agreed sum on the policyholder's death to beneficiaries specified in the policy.

Where the beneficiaries are the policyholder's spouse/children, s 11 MWPA 1882 requires the sum assured to be held on trust for them so that it does not become part of the policyholder's estate on his death but passes directly to them.

Nominations

A person who is entitled to funds which are in the hands of some other party may specify in his will that on his death these funds should be paid to a particular beneficiary.

In appropriate cases, the same object may be achieved by means of a nomination. This is a written direction by a person entitled to certain funds (the nominator) to the party holding these funds to pay such funds on the nominator's death, to some other person (the nominee). A nomination may be statutory or non-statutory.

Statutory nominations

These fall into two broad categories:

- Nominations which must not exceed £5,000. These include:
  - nominations by trade union members in respect of union benefits due to them; and
  - nominations by persons with savings in Friendly/Provident Societies or the Trustee Savings Bank.
- Nominations made before May 1981 by depositors in National Savings Bank accounts and investors in National Savings Certificates. These are not subject to the £5,000 limit.

Non-statutory nominations

Such nominations are usually made in the context of contributory pension schemes. The rules of these pension schemes normally provide that if a member dies before his retirement, certain benefits shall be paid to any person nominated by him (see Re *Danish Bacon Co Ltd* (1971) and *Baird v Baird* (1990)).

Nominations differ from wills in several respects:

- a nomination can be made by any person over 16, while a will is valid only if the testator has attained majority (see s 7 WA);
- the formalities which must be observed in making a nomination are determined not by the WA but by the relevant statute in the case of statutory nominations or the pension scheme rules in the cases of non-statutory ones;

- a nomination cannot be revoked by a subsequent will or codicil but only by a subsequent nomination. Moreover if the nominator has also left a will, *Bennet v Slater* (1889) establishes that the assets covered by the nomination will not constitute part of his estate but will go directly to the nominee.

Donatio mortis causa (DMC)

A DMC is a gift made in the donor's lifetime, which is expressed to be conditional upon and intended to take effect on his death. It is neither an *inter vivos* gift in the proper sense, nor is it a full-fledged testamentary gift (see *Re Beaumont* (1902)).

Three conditions must exist for a DMC to be valid:

- the gift must have been made in contemplation of the donor's impending death;
- the donor must intend the property to revert to him if the contemplated death does not occur; and
- the property (or the means of gaining control of it) must be delivered to the prospective donee.

Where the property is a chattel which has been delivered to the donee or he has been given the means of gaining access to it (eg the key to the place where it is kept), it passes directly to the donee on the donor's death (see, eg *Re Lillingstone* (1952) and *Woodard v Woodard* (1995)).

On the other hand, where the subject-matter of a DMC is a chose in action, land or other property which cannot be transferred by mere delivery, it passes on the donor's death to his personal representative and not to the donee. Equity will, however, compel the personal representative to vest the property in the donee despite the fact that the gift was not made by will (see, eg *Duffield v Elwes* (1827); *Re Wasserberg* (1915) and *Sen v Headley* (1991)).

2 The requirements of a valid will

Two basic requirements must be fulfilled before a will is valid:

- Compliance with the formalities prescribed in the WA;
- The mental capacity to make a will.

The formalities

A will is valid only if it is made in accordance with s 9 WA.

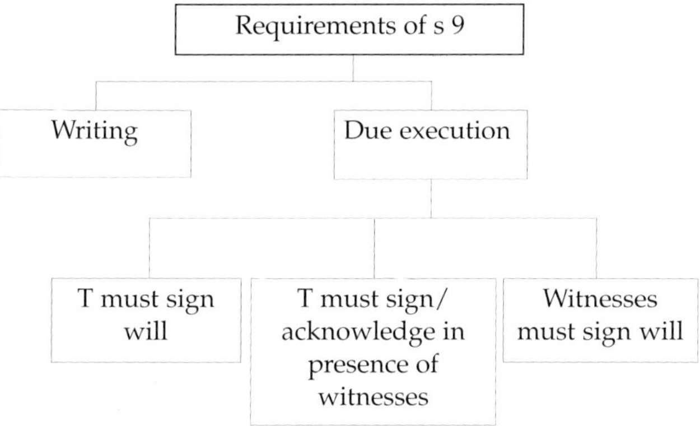

Whereas the requirement of writing has remained uniform since s 9 was originally enacted in 1837, the rules governing due execution have been altered in certain significant respects by s 17 AJA 1982 which introduced an amended s 9 into the WA.

The original s 9 still applies where T died before January 1983, while the amended s 9 now applies where T died after 1982.

The element of writing

While writing is demanded by s 9, as Buckley LJ points out in *Re Berger,* a will is not required 'to assume any particular form or to be couched in [technical] language'. Consequently:

- a simple home-made document framed in familiar everyday terms may constitute a valid will (see, eg *Thorn v Dickens* (1906) where the will simply read 'All for mother';
- there is no rule that a will must be in English. Thus, for instance, the courts have recognised the validity of;
    - a will in French: see *Whiting v Turner* (1903);
    - a will in Hebrew: see *Re Berger*; and
    - a will written partly in code: see *Kell v Charmer* (1856).

No mode of writing is prescribed in s 9 and accordingly wills may be handwritten, typewritten, wordprocessed or on standard printed forms which are usually available from stationers.

A handwritten will (or holograph) may be in ink or pencil. Where both ink and pencil are used and there is a conflict between the words in ink and those in pencil, the presumption is that the words in pencil were merely deliberative and not intended to operate as part of the will (see *In the Goods of Adams* (1872)).

The will can be written on any material. Thus, in *Hodson v Barnes* (1926), a will written on an empty egg shell was accepted as valid. It is, however, customary for the writing to be on paper (the format recommended for probate purposes being black wording on white A4 or foolscap paper).

The elements of due execution

The testator's signature

Under s 9, T is required to sign his will. Alternatively, it may be signed by someone else in T's presence and by his direction (see, eg *Smith v Harris* (1845) and *In the Goods of Clarke* (1839)).

While T usually inserts his name or usual signature on his will, the courts have tended to accept as sufficient any form of words or mark associated with T. See, eg:

Case	Accepted signature
In the Goods of Chalcraft (1948)	First four letters of T's surname where she was too ill to write her full name.
In the Estate of Cook (1960)	'Your loving mother' instead of T's name.
In the Goods of Savory (1851)	T's initials.
Re Jenkins (1863)	Rubber stamp bearing T's name.
Re Flinn (1935)	T's thumb print.

Summary of changes in the rules governing position of signature

Relevant period	Applicable statute	Criteria for validity of T's signature
1837–52	Original s 9	Will would fail unless T's signature was 'at the foot or end thereof'
1852–1982	Wills Act (Amendment) Act 1852	'Foot or end' of will given extended meaning to cover situations in which: • T's signature was not at the foot or end of the will but was inserted after or beside or opposite the end; • T's signature was separated from the end of the will by a blank space; • T's signature was inserted on a fresh page not containing any part of the will
1983 to date	Amended s 9	Signature on any part of will now suffices, provided it was intended to give effect to the will

The original s 9

Under the original s 9, T's signature had to appear at the *foot or end* of a will. This led to unsatisfactory results in cases like *Smee v Bryer* (1848) where a will was declared invalid because the signature was not on the tiny space at the bottom of the will but on a fresh page.

The Wills Act (Amendment) Act 1852

In response, Parliament enacted the Wills Act (Amendment) Act 1852. which provided that a signature which was positioned at/after/following/under/beside/opposite the end of the will would be valid once it was apparent that the testator intended by signing to give effect to the will.

It further provided that a signature would not be invalidated:

- because there was a blank space between the end of the will and the signature; or
- because it was made on a page on which no part of the will was written, even if the previous page contained sufficient space for the signature (as was the case in *Smee v Bryer*).

The practical operation of the Act is illustrated by *Re Roberts* (1927). The end of T's will had no space for a signature and so he placed his signature in the left hand margin. The signature was held to be opposite the end of the will and thus valid. In *In the Goods of Hornby* (1946), T's signature which was in an oblong box halfway down the page on which his will was written was held to be valid since T intended the box to be the end of his will.

The amended s 9

By contrast, *Re Stalman* (1931) decided that the 1852 Act did not validate a signature on the top right hand corner of a will. However, it can be deduced from *Wood v Smith* (1991) that *Stalman* would be decided differently if T had died after 1982, since the matter would then be governed by the amended s 9 which does not restrict T's signature to any part of the will.

The signature must be intended to give effect to the will: This requirement dates back to the 1852 Act and has been incorporated into the amended s 9.

If it appears that T did not intend his signature to give effect to his will, this causes the will to fail. In *In the Estate of Bean* (1944), T placed his unsigned will in an envelope and wrote his name and address on the envelope. The court found that the writing on the envelope was meant to identify its contents and not to give effect to the will, which was therefore invalid. This was followed in *Re Beadle* (1974) where T signed his will in the presence of one witness and then put it in an envelope which he signed before two witnesses. T's signature on the will had no effect as it was not properly witnessed while his signature on the envelope was held to be invalid on the same ground as in *Bean*.

Conversely, once it is established that a testator wrote his name or signature with the intention of giving effect to his will, this renders the will valid even if the name/signature appears on the envelope containing the will (as in *In the Goods of Mann* (1942)) or in the opening sentence of the will (as in *Wood v Smith*).

Witnessing the testator's signature

In order for a will to be duly executed, T's signature must be witnessed in the manner stipulated in s 9 which requires him to sign the will or acknowledge his signature in the presence of at least two persons who must be present at the same time.

Signature in the presence of witnesses: T's signature is valid, once the act of signing is witnessed by two persons. This is the case, even where:

- T does not tell these witnesses that the document being signed was his will (see *Re Benjamin* (1934));
- the signature is not actually visible to the witnesses (see *Smith v Smith* (1866)).

It has, however, been held in *Brown v Skirrow* (1902) that if there are two persons in a room with T when he signs his will but one of the two has not in fact observed T in the act of signing, T's signature will not be valid.

Acknowledgment in the presence of witnesses: If no witnesses are present when T signs, he must acknowledge his signature in the presence of witnesses. Cases like *Hudson v Parker* (1844), *Blake v Blake* (1882) and *Re Groffman* (1969) held that such an acknowledgment will be effective only if the witnesses actually see or had the opportunity to see T's signature on the will. (Contrast this with the position where T signs in the presence of witnesses.)

Modes of acknowledgment: Acknowledgment may be by words, eg if T produces a will bearing a signature which he declares is his. Acknowledgment may also be by gestures as seen from *In the Goods of Davies* (1850) and *In the Goods of Ouston* (1862). The courts have, in fact, gone so far as to accept that acknowledgment may occur where T places his will before the witnesses with his signature being visible and asks them to sign it, even if he does not signify by words or gestures that the signature is his (see *Keigwin v Keigwin* (1843) and *Daintree v Butcher* (1888)).

The witnesses' signatures

After T signed his will or acknowledged his signature in the presence of witnesses, they in turn, were required by the old s 9 to subscribe (ie sign the will) in T's presence.

No provision was made in the old s 9 for a witness to sign beforehand and later acknowledge his signature in the testator's presence. One notable consequence of this, as seen from cases like *Wyatt v Berry* (1893) and *Re Colling* (1972), was that if T signed his will in the presence of a witness (W1) who then signed and T thereafter acknowledged his signature in the presence of W1 and another witness (W2) after which W2 signed, the will would not be valid unless W1 also signed again. An acknowledgment of his earlier signature would not suffice.

The position has now been altered where T dies after 1982 by the amended s 9 which provides for acknowledgment by witnesses. This is reflected in *Couser v Couser* (1996) where T acknowledged his signature before W1 who then signed. W2 later joined T and W1 in the room and they both acknowledged their signatures whereupon W2 then signed the will. The will was held to be valid.

Where it is claimed that a witness signed in T's presence but T was not in a position to see the witness in the act of signing, this invalidates the will. See, eg *Wright v Manifold* where T signed the will and the witnesses then signed it in an adjoining room out of T's line of vision. But note: that even if T is not in the room where the witnesses sign the will but he is able to observe them signing it (eg through an open window), the will is valid as established by *Casson v Dade* (1781).

In the same way as T, a witness may sign by inserting his name, signature, initials, thumbprint or other mark on the will; or may identify himself by description as in *In the Goods of Sperling* (1863) where a witness signed as 'Servant to Mr Sperling'.

Incorporation of unexecuted documents into duly executed wills

A document which has not been executed in accordance with s 9 is deemed to constitute part of a duly executed will, once it has been incorporated by reference into that will.

Requirements for incorporation		
Document must be in existence	Will must refer to document as being in existence	Document must be identified sufficiently in will

The law imposes three conditions for incorporation by reference:

- The document being incorporated must be in existence when the will is executed (see *Singleton v Tomlinson* (1878)). But note the decision in *In the Goods of Truro* (1866) that where the document comes into being after the will is executed but that will is later republished, this condition is satisfied since the will is deemed to have been executed on the date of republication.
- The will must refer to the document as being in existence. Where a will refers to a document without specifying that it is in existence at the time the will was made there can be no incorporation as can be seen from *University College of North Wales v Taylor* (1908) (where the will referred to 'any memorandum ... written or signed by me') and in *In the Goods of Sutherland* (1866) (where it referred to 'any existing or future document signed by me').
- The reference in the will to a document must be clear enough to enable the document to be identified (see *In the Goods of Garnett* (1898)). Parole evidence is, however, admissible to identify the document where the will is not sufficiently explicit (see *Allen v Maddock* (1858)).

Privileged wills

Under s 11 WA as amended by the Wills (Soldiers and Sailors) Act 1918, the requirement of due execution does not apply to wills made by certain categories of privileged testators, notably:

Soldiers in actual military service

In addition to full-time combat soldiers, this category encompasses:

Re Rowson (1944) *Re Wingham* (1949)	Air Force personnel.
Re Rippon (1943)	Territorial Army officers.
In the Estate of Stanley (1944)	Members of support units, eg medical corps, chaplaincy.

A soldier is privileged only when *in actual military service*. This was construed by Lord Denning in *Re Wingham* to mean that he must be engaged in 'military operations which are or have been taking place or are believed to be imminent'. Later cases have accepted that a soldier may be in actual military service even where the nation is not at war. See, eg *In the Estate of Colman* (1958) (soldier serving with British Army on the Rhine) and *Re Jones* (1981) (soldier posted to Northern Ireland).

Mariners or seamen being at sea

This category includes those serving in the Royal Navy, Royal Marines or Merchant Navy. The capacity in which they are serving does not matter once the nature of their job involves going to sea. See, eg *In the Goods of Hale* (1916) (female typist on ocean liner); and *In the Estate of Knibbs* (1962) (barman on ocean liner).

A mariner or seaman is privileged only while at sea. He is deemed to be at sea not only where he has actually set sail but also where he has not yet embarked on his journey but is preparing to do so, having received his orders to join ship (see *In the Goods of Hale*; *Re Newland's Estate* (1952) and *Re Wilson's Estate* (1952)) (but contrast with *Re Rapley's Estate* (1983) which held that a will made days before a sailor received orders was not privileged).

The courts have also held that a sailor or mariner was at sea where his ship was:

- permanently stationed in Portsmouth: *In the Goods of M'Murdo* (1868);
- moored on the Thames ready to sail: *Re Patterson* (1898);
- sailing on the Rangoon river: *Re Austen* (1853);
- docked in a foreign port: *In the Goods of Lay* (1840).

Members of HM's naval or marine forces so circumstanced that if they were soldiers they would be in actual military service

This third category was included by the W(SS)A and was designed to ensure that officers and men of the Royal Navy and Royal Marines (but not the Merchant Navy) could make privileged wills in all situations where soldiers were entitled to do so (see *In the Estate of Yates* (1919)).

Characteristics of privileged wills

Privileged wills differ from ordinary wills in a variety of respects. In particular:

- Privileged wills need not comply with the formalities in s 9. It follows that an oral statement may qualify as a privileged will (see *In the Estate of Yates*; *Re Stable* (1919) and *Re Jones*). Equally, a written statement which is not signed or witnessed may constitute a privileged will (see *In the Goods of Hale* and *In the Estate of Stanley*).

  Such an oral or written statement will not amount to a privileged will unless the maker evinced a firm intention that his property should devolve in the stated manner. It was for this reason that the court in *In the Estate of Knibbs* refused to treat as a privileged will a casual remark by K to a fellow barman on his ship that if he died, all he owned would pass to his sister.

- A non-privileged testator cannot revoke his will by another will, unless the latter is also duly executed. By contrast, a privileged testator may revoke his will by an informal privileged will. This is the case not only where the will being revoked is a privileged will but also where it is a duly executed will (as was the case in *In the Estate of Gossage* (1921)).

  On the issue of revocation it is also noteworthy that:

  - a privileged will made by a person who then ceases to be privileged can only be revoked by a later will if the latter is duly executed;

  - marriage operates to revoke a privileged will (as was the case in *In the Estate of Wardrop* (1917)); while a written privileged will (but not an oral one) can also be revoked by destruction;

  - where a privileged will is not revoked by any of these methods, it remains effective even if the testator had ceased to be privileged long before he died (see *Re Booth* (1926)).

- The stipulation in s 7 WA that a will executed by a minor is void does not apply where the minor is a privileged testator (see *Re Newland's Estate).*
- Privileged wills are not subject to the rule in s 15 WA which provides that beneficiary loses his entitlement if he or his spouse witnesses the will (see *Re Limond* (1915)).

Testamentary capacity

A will is valid only if T possessed the requisite testamentary capacity at the time he made it.

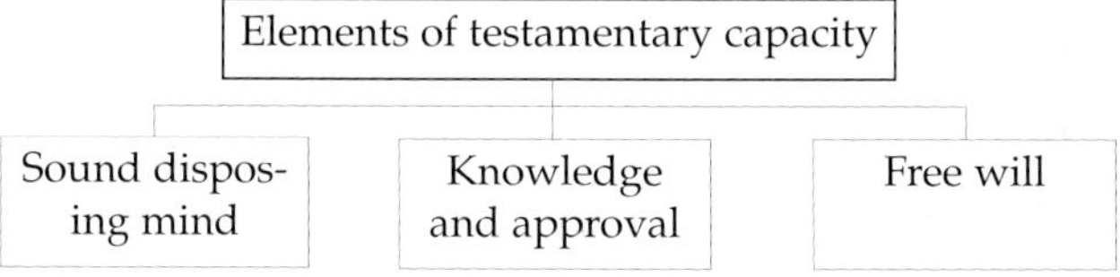

Sound disposing mind

T can only make a will if he is of sound disposing mind. As seen from *Banks v Goodfellow* (1870), this requirement is fulfilled if:

- T understands the nature and effect of making a will;
- T understands the extent of the property being disposed of;
- T is aware of those who have claims to his estate; and
- T is not suffering from a disease of mind or insane delusion which distorts his judgment.

The criteria set out in *Banks v Goodfellow* were aptly summarised by Hannen P who stated in *Boughton v Knight* (1873) that soundness of mind consists of two vital components, namely; soundness of understanding and soundness of memory.

Soundness of understanding

Delusions which influence contents of T's will

Mental illness/insanity

Subnormal intelligence

Conditions which may provide evidence of lack of understanding on the part of T

Brain damage resulting from accidents

Intoxication or drug intake

Senile dementia and other degenerative illnesses

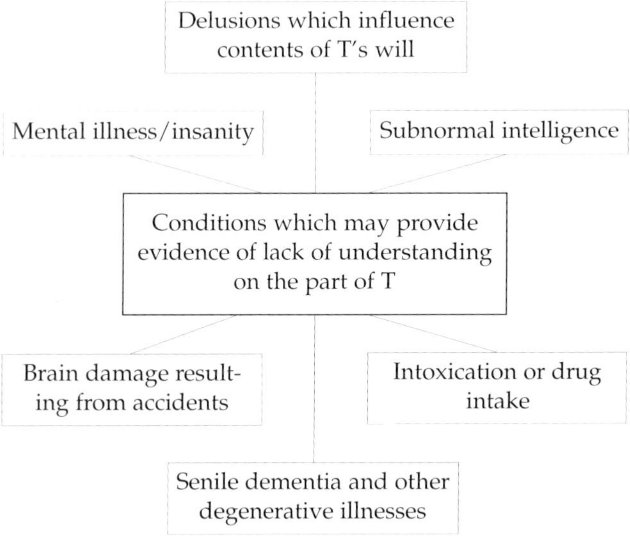

T must be capable of understanding what he is doing when making his will. A will is thus liable to fail if, at the time of making it, T's mind was impaired by some disease or defect which made it unlikely that he would appreciate the significance of his act. This may happen, for instance where:

- T was born with substantially subnormal intelligence;

- T is a mental patient or lunatic with a severe mental disorder;
- T had suffered an injury which caused damage to his brain;
- T's mind is impaired by senility or other degenerative illness.

  Note: If T is elderly, it is advisable when executing his will for a doctor to examine his mental state and act as a witness (see *Kenward v Adams* (1975) and *Re Simpson* (1977)).

- T made the will at a time when his mind had been altered by drink or drugs (see *Ayrey v Hill* (1924); *Brunt v Brunt* (1873) and *Re Heinke's Estate* (1959)).
- T, while being sane in most respects, suffers from a specific delusion which affects his judgment to a degree which affects the dispositions which he makes in his will (see *Banks v Goodfellow*; *Dew v Clarke* (1826); *Re Bellis* (1929) and *Re Nightingale* (1974)).

Soundness of memory

T must have sufficient recollection of the extent of his estate and the nature of the property he seeks to dispose of (see *Waters v Waters* (1848) and *Re Beaney* (1978)).

Moreover, if T is unable to recollect those persons he is ordinarily obliged to provide, his will is invalid (see *Boughton v Knight* (1873) and *Battan Singh v Amirchand* (1948)). But *note*, however, *Harwood v Baker* (1840) where it was pointed out that, that this will not be the case if T is well aware of the persons who have a moral claim on his bounty, but nevertheless deliberately forms an intelligent purpose to exclude such persons from any share in his property.

The degree of soundness

The courts do not insist that T must exhibit the highest level of soundness of mind in order to be capable of making a will. What is required is that he must be able to discern and judge, as they apply to his situation, all those matters and circumstances which go into making a will. It follows that the question of soundness is dealt with in relation to the facts and subject-matter of each case and in particular, the simplicity or complexity of the will being executed (see *Re Park's Estate* (1954)).

When must the testamentary capacity be present?

T is required to be of sound mind at the time he executes the will.

This requirement has, however, been relaxed in one specific context by the rule in *Parker v Felgate* (1883). This rule stipulates that if T, while being of sound mind, instructed a solicitor to prepare his will but was no longer of sound mind when executing it, the will is adjudged to be valid, provided:

- it was duly prepared according to T's instructions; and
- at the time of execution, T was able to understand that he was executing a will prepared pursuant to his instructions, even if he no longer remembered what the instructions were or understood the true import of the dispositions in the will.

At the same time, however, the courts are reluctant to pronounce a will valid on the strength of the rule in *Parker v Felgate*, where the evidence discloses that it was executed in suspicious circumstances as was the case in *Battan Singh v Amirchand*.

Proof of capacity

According to Parke B in *Barry v Butlin* (1838), the party who seeks to establish the validity of a will must prove that T had the requisite mental capacity.

Where direct evidence is available regarding T's mental state, the issue is decided on the basis of such evidence. If such evidence is unavailable, the courts invoke two presumptions:

- *Rationality*: If a will appears on its face to be rational, T is presumed to have been sane when executing it and the burden rests on the party contesting its validity to prove otherwise (see *Wellesley v De Vere* (1841) and *Symes v Greene* (1859)).

  If the will is irrational on its face, T is presumed not to have been of sound mind, and the burden of proving otherwise lies with the party propounding the will. The matter is, however, complicated by cases like *Mudway v Croft* (1843); *Frere v Peacocke* (1846) and *Pilkington v Gray* (1899) which have acknowledged that signs of eccentricity in T's will do not in themselves signify a lack of mental capacity. The difficulty here is in distinguishing between eccentricity and the sort of irrationality that raises the presumption against soundness of mind. As a general guide, it was suggested in *Mudway* that eccentricity had to be judged against T's whole life and habits, such that a disposition which on the face of it might appear irrational might in the light of his lifestyle and habits be attributed to his eccentricity.

- *Continuance of a mental state:* Where there is evidence that T was in full command of his faculties some time before making his will, he is presumed to have had a sound disposing mind when he executed it (see *Chambers and Yatman v Queen's Proctor* (1840)).

Conversely, where there is evidence that T was unsound in mind some time before making the will, the presumption is that this was also the case at the time he executed it (see *Smee v Smee* (1879) and *Banks v Goodfellow*). The party seeking to propound the will, may, however, rebut this presumption by proving that T executed it either after recovery or during a lucid interval (see *Chambers and Yatman* and *Re Walker's Estate* (1912)).

Knowledge and approval

Even where T was undoubtedly of sound mind, a will may nevertheless be invalid if it appears that he did not know and approve of its contents. Such a possibility is especially pronounced where T executes a will prepared for him by some other person.

Proving knowledge and approval

The onus of proving knowledge and approval lies with the party propounding the will.

The basic presumption

Where T was of sound mind and his will was duly executed, he is presumed to have known and approved of its contents (see *Barry v Butlin*; *Guardhouse v Blackburn* (1866) and *Cleare v Cleare* (1869)).

Situations in which knowledge and approval will not be presumed:

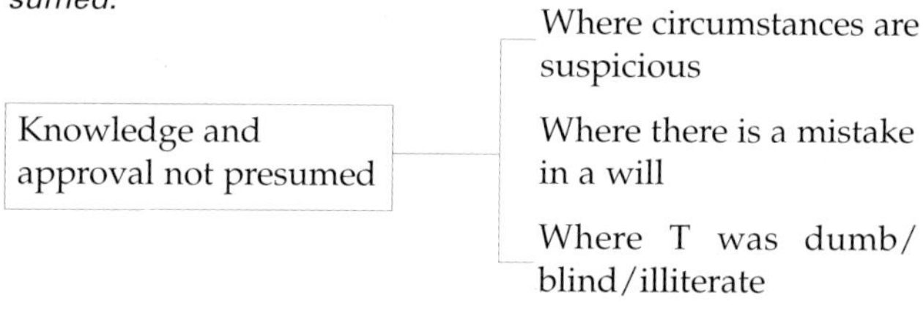

Knowledge and approval not presumed

- Where circumstances are suspicious
- Where there is a mistake in a will
- Where T was dumb/blind/illiterate

Suspicious circumstances

The most obvious situation in which suspicions are aroused is where a will is prepared by a person who receives substantial benefits thereunder. Where this happens, the onus is on that person to prove T's knowledge and approval. If he is unable to do so, it has been held in cases like *Fulton v Andrew* (1875) and *Wintle v Nye* (1959) that this invalidates either the entire will or the gift in favour of such a person.

It was, however, emphasised in *Barry v Butlin* that it is not in every case where a person who prepared a will receives a benefit that this raises sufficient suspicion to require him to prove T's knowledge and approval. For example, there is little ground for suspicion if a will prepared by a solicitor for a wealthy and experienced businessperson contains a modest legacy in the solicitor's favour.

Other situations which gives rise to suspicion are:

- where the recipient of a substantial benefit did not prepare the will but was active in some other respect (eg taking T to a solicitor chosen by him or relaying T's wishes to T's solicitor, see *Brown v Fisher* (1890) and *Bhattan Singh v Amirchand*);
- where the party who prepared the will did not himself receive any benefit but a close relation of his was a substantial beneficiary (see *Tyrell v Painton* (1894); *Thomas v Jones* (1928); *Re Ticehurst* (1973) and *Re A Solicitor* (1975)).

The position where the will has been read over: It was accepted in cases like *Guardhouse v Blackburn* and *Atter v Atkinson* that if a will which was executed in suspicious circumstances was then read by or to T, this was sufficient proof that he knew and approved of its contents. This view has now been called into question in *Re Morris* (1971) where Latey J declared that it 'does not survive in any shape or form' as a strict rule.

Mistake

Where T was labouring under a material mistake when he executed his will, this may operate to displace the presumption that he knew and approved of its contents.

Such a mistake may arise, for instance, where a will prepared for T1 is executed by T2 while T1 executes a will prepared for T2, as was the case *In the Goods of Hunt* (1875) and *Re Meyer's Estate* (1908). A mistake of this nature renders both wills invalid.

Mistakes in a will may also result from the unintended inclusion of certain words or provisions in the will or unintended omission of words or clauses which T had wanted to include in the will.

Unintended inclusion: The court may rectify the will by ordering it to be read as if the words which were mistakenly included had been deleted (see *Re Phelan* (1972)).

But *note* that there will be no rectification where T intended particular words to be included in his will but was mistaken as to the legal effect of such words (see *Collins v Elstone* (1893)).

Unintended omission: It was established in cases like *Re Boehm* (1891), *Re Morris* and *Re Reynette-James* (1976) that where a will mistakenly omitted certain words which T had intended to include, the court had no power to rectify it by ordering their inclusion.

By virtue of s 20(1) AJA, the courts now possess a limited power to rectify omissions which were due to clerical errors or failure to understand instructions (see *Wordingham v Royal Exchange Trust Co* (1992)). The courts may also have recourse to s 20 when dealing with applications to delete words which were mistakenly included in a will (see *Re Segelman (Deceased)* (1995)).

Dumb, blind and illiterate testators

Where a dumb testator executes a will prepared for him by another person, the courts require evidence that he knew and approved of its contents (see *In the Goods of Geale* (1864); *In the Goods of Owston* (1862) and *In the Estate of Holtam* (1913)).

Evidence of knowledge and approval is also required where the testator is blind or illiterate (see *Fincham v Edwards* (1842) and *Christian v Instiful* (1954)). This requirement is usually satisfied by the inclusion of an attestation clause which declares that the blind/illiterate testator signed the will after it had been read to him in the presence of the witnesses and he appeared to have understood and approved of it.

Free will

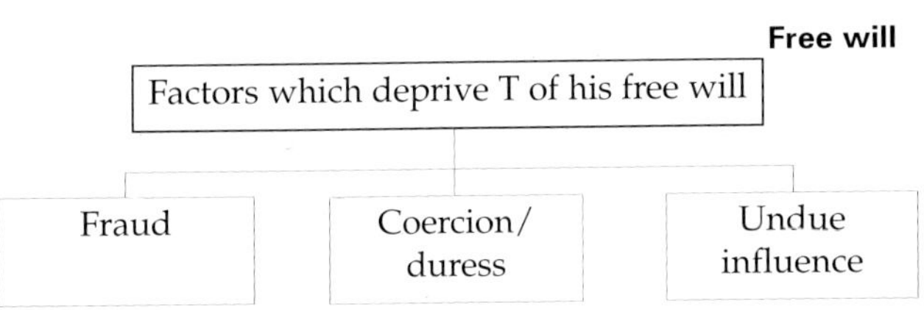

Fraud

Where T is fraudulently induced to dispose of his property by will in a particular manner, this may be challenged on the ground that it is not the product of T's free will. See *Butterfield v Scawen* (1775) where T amended his will to disinherit B after being misinformed that B had tried to poison him; and *Wilkinson v Joughin* (1866) where T made a will in favour of B who had tricked him into marrying her even though she was already married.

Coercion and undue influence

Where T is coerced into making his will in a particular manner by the application or threat of force, this invalidates the will or that part of it which he was coerced into making.

Where no force or threats have been employed, but undue influence of a more subtle kind has been exerted against T, this may also invalidate his will. In *Wingrove v Wingrove* (1885), for instance, the court made it clear that if at a time when T was dying, he was pestered into making his will in a particular manner, such a will would be tainted by undue influence. Again, in *Re Harden* (1959) undue influence was found to be present where T left most of her estate to B, a spiritualist medium acting on the strength of messages which B claimed to have received from the spirit world. Similarly, in *Simpson v Simpson* (1989), where T, having become completely reliant on his third wife B after developing a malignant brain tumour, transferred most of his wealth to B in his lifetime and provided in his will that the rest of his estate was to pass to B, these dispositions were invalid because B was found to have exerted undue influence.

Where *persuasion* which falls short of undue influence is employed to obtain a benefit under a will, this does not render the will invalid. Commenting on the distinction between persuasion and undue influence, Lord Penzance signified in *Hall v Hall* (1868) that 'persuasion suggests an appeal to the affections or ties of kindred, to a sentiment of gratitude for past services or pity for future destitution or the like; whereas undue influence involves the application of pressure of whatever character, whether acting on the fears or the hopes, so ... as to overpower the volition without convincing the judgment'.

The burden of proving fraud and undue influence: While it is incumbent on a person seeking to propound a will to show that it was made with T's knowledge and approval, it is not for him to prove the absence of fraud or undue influence. Instead, any party who pleads fraud or undue influence must furnish the necessary proof.

Such a plea should not be made lightly since cases like *Craig v Lamourex* (1920) and *Re Cutliffe's Estate* (1959) show that very strong evidence is required before it can be upheld. In line with this principle, the court held in *Parfit v Lawless* (1872) where T left her entire estate to B, her chaplain and personal confessor, their relationship did not in itself raise a presumption that B had unduly influenced T and further proof was needed in order to establish such undue influence.

3 Revocation, alteration, revival and republication of wills

Revocation

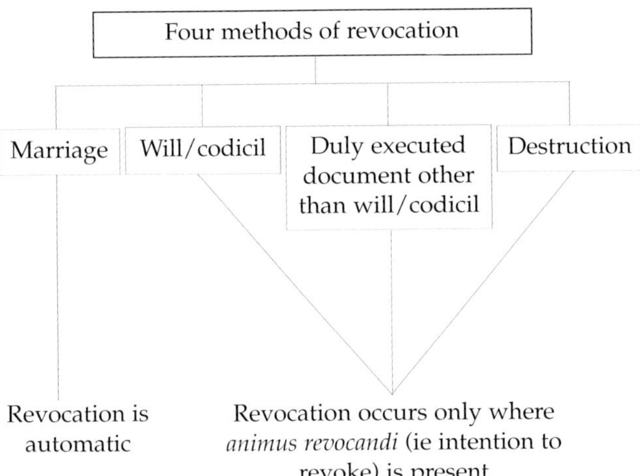

Revocation by marriage

General rule

Under s 18(1) WA, marriage operates to revoke any prior will made by either spouse. This is so not only where the marriage is valid but also where it is voidable under s 12 MCA (1973) (as can be seen from *Re Roberts* (1978)); but not if it was void *ab initio* (as was the case in *Mette v Mette* (1859) and *De Reneville v De Reneville* (1948)).

Exceptions

There are two notable exceptions to this rule:

Wills made in expectation of marriage

This exception was introduced by s 177 LPA (1925) which provided that a will expressed to be in contemplation of marriage would not be revoked by the solemnisation of that marriage.

For the purpose of s 177, a will was deemed to be in contemplation of marriage, not only where T expressly referred to his imminent marriage as the reason for making it, but also in cases like *Re Knight* (1944) and *Re Langston* (1953) where T left his whole estate to a lady named in his will as his fiancee or future wife.

However, in *Re Coleman* (1976), where T left a sizeable part of his estate to M who he named in his will as his fiancee and the rest to his brother and sister, it was held that the will was not made in contemplation of marriage within the meaning of s 177 and was thus revoked by T's subsequent marriage to M.

This decision has been criticised not least by the Law Reform Committee in its 'Report on the Making and Revocation of Wills' which prompted Parliament to repeal s 177 with effect from January 1983 and to enact in its place s 18(3) and (4) WA.

Section 18(3) provides that where it appears from a will that at the time it was made T was expecting to be married to a particular person and intended that the will should not be revoked by that marriage, the will shall not be revoked by such marriage.

For its part, s 18(4) reverses the effect of the *Coleman* decision by providing that where it appears from a will that at the time it was made T was expecting to be married to a particular person and that he intended that *a disposition in the will* should not be revoked by his marriage to that person, that disposition shall take effect in spite of the marriage; and any other disposition shall also take effect unless it appears from the will that T intended it to be revoked.

Where the testator employs the will to exercise a power of appointment
Section 18(2) WA provides that a disposition in a will in the exercise of a power of appointment conferred on T, is not revoked by T's marriage unless the property appointed would in default of appointment pass to his personal representatives.

Revocation by subsequent will or codicil
Under s 20 WA, if T intends to revoke his will in whole or in part he may do so by executing a will or codicil.

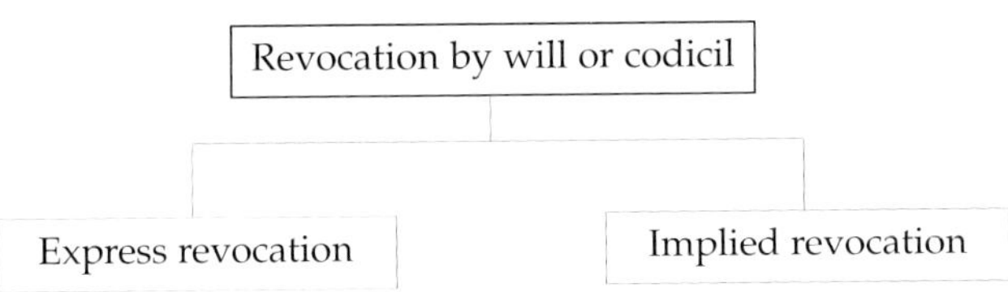

Express revocation
Most wills contain a general clause revoking all previous testamentary dispositions made by T.

Some wills/codicils contain more specific clauses which are expressed to revoke only particular provisions or dispositions. See, eg *In the Estate of Wayland* (1951) where T inserted a revocation clause intended to deal with his estate in England as distinct from his property in Belgium.

An express revocation clause appearing in a will is of no effect:

- where T did not know and approve of its inclusion in the will (see *Re Phelan* (1972); but contrast with *Collins v Elstone* (1893));
- where the clause appears in a conditional will or codicil which does not come into force because the condition is not fulfilled (see *In the Estate of O'Connor* (1942)); and
- where the intention to revoke is itself conditional and the underlying condition is not fulfilled.

Implied revocation

A will or codicil with no express revocation clause can impliedly revoke a previous will/codicil either:

- where the later will/codicil merely repeats the provisions of the earlier one, in which case the court will simply treat it as a substitute for the earlier one (see *Dempsey v Lawson* (1877)); or
- where the earlier will and the later one contain provisions which are mutually inconsistent.

Where such inconsistency or repetition is partial, any parts of the earlier will which are consistent with or not repeated in the later will remain unrevoked (see *Lemage v Goodban* (1865); *In the Goods of Petchell* (1874) and *Re Bund* (1929)).

Where the provisions of the two wills are wholly inconsistent or repetitive, the earlier one is totally revoked by the later one (see *Cadell v Wilcocks* (1898) and *In the Estate of Bryan* (1907)).

A problem may arise where there are two inconsistent wills and it is impossible to tell which is later either because they are both undated or because they both bear the same date. In such a case neither will can be admitted to probate (see *Re Howard* (1994)).

Revocation by some other document

Under s 20, a will or codicil may be revoked not only by a later will or codicil but also by 'some writing declaring an intention to revoke and duly executed in the same manner as a will'. This method of revocation has been judicially recognised in *In the Goods of Durance* (1872) and *Re Spracklan's Estate* (1938).

Revocation by destruction

In addition, s 20 provides for a will or codicil to be revoked by burning, tearing or otherwise destroying it with the intention of revoking it.

Although s 20 mentions two specific modes of destruction (burning and tearing), the inclusion of the words 'otherwise destroying' signifies that other similar acts will suffice, eg cutting up the will or removing vital portions such as T's signature with scissors or a knife (see *Hobbs v Knight* (1836) and *In the Goods of Morton* (1887)).

But in *Cheese v Lovejoy* (1887), where T drew some lines across his will and wrote on the back that it was revoked before throwing it on a pile of waste paper from which a servant later rescued it, it was held that this was not a sufficient act of destruction (see also *In the Goods of Brewster* (1859)). Contrast with *Re Adams,* where T directed her solicitor to destroy her will but he sent it back to her to do so herself. On receiving the will, T scored out her signature and those of the witnesses with a ball point pen so that they were no longer visible to the naked eye. It was held that the will had been revoked by destruction.

Partial destruction

Where T destroys only a portion of the will, the will is only partially revoked, such that the portion that was not destroyed shall take effect on T's death (see *Re Everest* (1975); *In the Goods Of Woodward* (1871) and *In the Estate of Nunn* (1936)).

Destruction by another person

The act of destruction may not be be carried out by T, but by another person in his presence and at his direction.

If the act of destruction is not done in T's presence, this does not operate to revoke the will (*In the Estate of De Kremer* (1965) and *In the Goods Of Dadds* (1857)).

Equally, where the destruction occurs in T's presence but without his consent, the will is not revoked (see *Mills v Millward* (1890) and *Gill v Gill* (1909).

Intention to revoke

T must have intended to revoke the will when the destruction took place. Accordingly, a will is not revoked:

- where T assumed in error that he was destroying a document other than his will; or
- when T was not of sound mind when the will was destroyed (see *Brunt v Brunt* (1873) and *Re Aynsley* (1973)).

T's intention to revoke must subsist until the mode of destruction chosen by him has been completed. For instance, if T sets out to destroy his will by tearing it into pieces, but after the first tear is restrained and persuaded not to continue, the will stands unrevoked (see *Doe D Perkes v Perkes* (1820)).

Presumptions

Two rebuttable presumptions apply in the context of revocation by destruction.

Presumption where will is missing

Where T made a will which was last known to be in his possession but it is missing at his death, he is presumed to have revoked it by destruction (see *Welch v Phillips* (1836) and *Re Ziggles* (1974)).

This presumption is, however, rebuttable where there is credible evidence to show that T did not seek to revoke the will but that it had in all probability been stolen, lost or misplaced (as in *Sugden v Lord St Leonards* (1876)) or destroyed by a bomb dropped on T's house during World War II (as in *Re Webb* (1964)).

Presumption where will is found mutilated

Where a will in T's possession at his death is torn or mutilated and there is no explanation as to how it got into this condition, it was held in *Lambell v Lambell* (1831) that revocation by destruction will be presumed. This is, however, difficult to reconcile with *Cowling v Cowling* (1924) which suggests that in such an event, the appropriate inference to draw is that T retained the will in spite of its condition because he intended it to take effect on his death.

In the final analysis, the presumption to be adopted may well depend on the extent of damage to the will. If it is considerable, it is reasonable to presume that T intended to revoke; whereas if it is slight, the converse presumption may be more appropriate.

Conditional revocation

Where T sets out to revoke a will by destruction or by a later will or other duly executed document, the intention to revoke may be *absolute* or *conditional*. If it is *absolute*, it suffices for one of these modes of revocation to be employed.

If it is conditional, it emerges from cases such as *Campbell v French* (1797) and *Re Carey* (1977) that the revocation will take effect only if, in addition, the material condition is satisfied.

The problem of whether revocation is absolute or conditional is especially acute in situations where T contemplates making other arrangements concerning the disposition of his property on death. In such cases, it is necessary to decide whether T intended:

- that the will would be revoked in any event; or
- that revocation was to be conditional on the disposition being valid. Such conditional revocation is also known as *dependent relative revocation*, although the aptness of this phrase has been called into question by various judges and academic commentators.

The courts have found it necessary to determine whether revocation is absolute or dependent on the validity of another disposition in a variety of contexts.

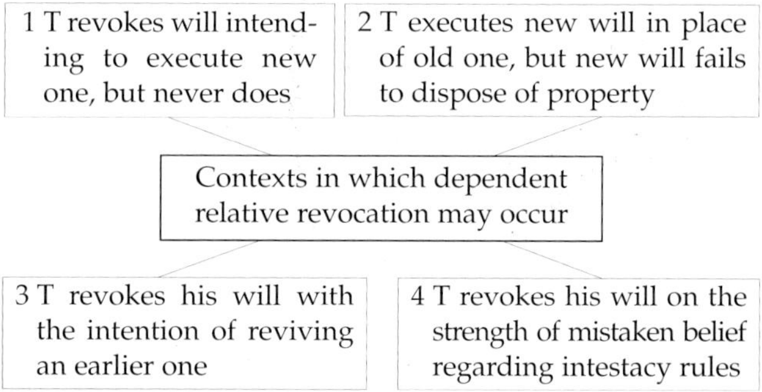

Contexts in which dependent relative revocation may occur

1 T revokes will intending to execute new one, but never does

2 T executes new will in place of old one, but new will fails to dispose of property

3 T revokes his will with the intention of reviving an earlier one

4 T revokes his will on the strength of mistaken belief regarding intestacy rules

Where T revokes his will with a view to making a new one but dies before the new will is made

In cases like *Dixon v Treasury Solicitor* (1905) and *In the Estate of Bronham* (1951), the courts decided that in such an event, T's revocation would be dependent on the making of the new will so that if he died before making the new will, the revocation of the earlier will would be of no effect.

It was, however, made clear in *Re Jones* (1976) that the fact that T revokes his will with a view to making another does not automatically make such revocation dependent on the new will being made.

Where T revokes his earlier will and makes a new one which does not effectively dispose of his property

Where T makes a later will in which he purports to revoke an earlier will, but for some reason the later will fails to dispose of his property, it has been held in cases like *Re Robinson* (1930); *In the Goods of Hope Brown* (1942) and *Re Finnemore* (1991) that the earlier will remains unrevoked, if in the court's view, its revocation was dependent on the later will being effective.

Where it happens that T makes the later will and either before or after executing it, revokes his earlier will by destruction, cases like *In the Goods of Middleton* (1864) and *Re Davies* (1928) have held that if the new will fails for any reason, the earlier one is deemed not to have been revoked if the court concludes that T intended the revocation to depend on the validity of the new will.

At the same time, it is evident from *In the Estate of Green* (1962) that the failure of the later will does not prevent such revocation by destruction from taking effect where there is evidence that T intended the revocation to be absolute rather than conditional on the validity of the later will.

Where T revokes his later will intending to revive an earlier one
Where T makes a new will revoking an earlier will and later on revokes this new will, this does not revive the earlier one.

However, if T, in revoking the new will, intended this to be conditional on the revival of the old one, it has been held in *Powell v Powell* (1866); *Cossey v Cossey* (1900); *Re Bridgewater's Estate* (1965) and *Re Janotta* (1976) that in the absence of the intended revival, the revocation of the later will is ineffective.

Where T revokes his will incorrectly believing that his estate will devolve in a particular manner on intestacy
Once the court finds that T revoked his will on the condition that his estate would devolve in a given manner, the will remains unrevoked if it emerges that the estate will devolve in a different manner under the prevailing intestacy rules (see *Re Southernden* (1925)).

Alteration of wills

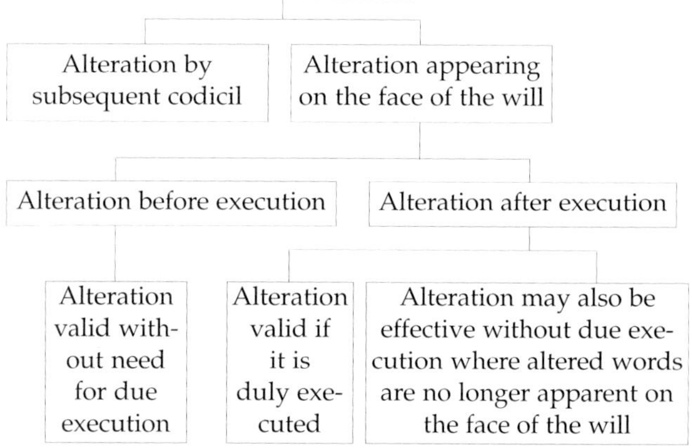

If T seeks to alter his will, he may either:

- execute a codicil setting out the desired amendments; or
- embody the proposed amendments in the will itself.

Our primary concern in the present context is with those alterations which are embodied in the will.

Alterations before execution

Where there is evidence that T altered his will before execution with the intention that this would form part of the will, the alteration is valid whether or not it was signed and attested.

There is, however, a rebuttable presumption that all alterations were made after a will and any codicils thereto were executed (see *Cooper v Bocket* (1846); *In the Goods of Adamson* (1875) and *In the Goods of Sykes* (1873)). If the presumption is not rebutted, an alteration will only be valid if T has complied with s 21 WA.

Rebuttal may be by internal evidence from the will itself of the type accepted in cases like *Birch v Birch* (1848); *In the Goods of Cadge* (1848) and *In the Goods of Hindmarsh* (1866). In other cases such as *Re Jacob's Goods* (1842) and *Keigwin v Keigwin* (1843), the presumption has been rebutted by adducing extrinsic evidence such as the testimony of an attesting witness.

Alterations after execution

These are governed by s 21 which provides that an obliteration, interlineation or other alteration made in a will after execution is capable of taking effect on either of two grounds, namely:

- where the alteration was duly executed like a will; or

- where as a result of the alteration, certain words in the will or the effect of parts of the will are no longer apparent.

Where the alteration has been duly executed

> An alteration in a duly executed will made after the execution thereof is not effective unless the alteration is executed in the manner required by statute for the execution of the will – *per* Buckley J in *Re Hay* (1904).

This means, in effect, that the alteration has to be signed by T and witnessed by two persons, though it is not clear whether they must be the original witnesses to the will. Section 21 specifies that the signature of T and his witnesses should either be made:

- in the margin or on some part of the will opposite or near the alteration; or
- if the will contains a memorandum referring to the alteration, at the foot or end or opposite the memorandum.

An issue which has not yet been fully resolved is whether an alteration made by T in the presence of witnesses and signed by these witnesses but not by T is deemed to be duly executed. In one line of cases typified by *In the Goods of Shearn* (1880) and *In Re White (Deceased)* (1991), the courts have refused to give effect to alterations made in such circumstances on the ground that they were not duly executed. By contrast, in *Re Dewell* (1853), it was decided that such an alteration had been duly executed because although it was not signed by T, in the court's view, his conduct at the time the alteration was made amounted to an acknowledgment of the signature he had put on the will when it was originally executed.

Academic opinion is also divided with Parry & Clark claiming that *Dewell* was wrongly decided, while Mellows appears to prefer the approach adopted in *Dewell* to that in *Shearn*.

Alterations by privileged testators

Since a privileged testator is able to make an informal will, it follows that he may also alter his will after execution, without the alteration being duly executed (see *In the Goods of Tweedale* (1874)).

Where the wording of the will is no longer apparent

If T wishes to alter his will by deleting some words or clauses, he may achieve this by obliterating them from the will. Provided this is done in such a manner that the original wording is no longer apparent on the face of the will, the desired alteration will take effect without being duly executed even if made after the will was executed (see *In the Goods of Hamer* (1944)).

On the other hand, where T seeks to delete some words or clauses from his previously executed will without completely obliterating them, so long as they are still apparent, the alteration will be valid only if it was duly executed.

The yardstick for determining whether words are 'apparent' on the face of the will is to determine whether they can still be deciphered by natural means simply by inspecting the will in the state in which T left it (see *In the Goods of Horsford* (1874) and *In the Goods of Ibbetsen* (1839)).

This means, in effect, that if the alteration has obscured certain words but they remain visible to the naked eye such words will still be read as part of the will. The words will also be read as part of the will where they can still be discerned by using a magnifying glass (as in *In the Goods of Braiser* (1899)); or by holding up the paper to the light with a brown paper frame around the portion being deciphered (as in *Ffinch v Combe* (1894)).

By contrast, the words are not considered to be apparent within the meaning of s 21 if they are decipherable only by artificial devices such as chemical agents (as in *In the Goods of Horsford*) or infra-red photography (as in *In the Goods of Itter* (1950)); or through physical interference such as the removal of a strip of paper pasted over a portion of the will.

The requirement of animus revocandi

The fact that certain words in a will have become so obliterated that a part of the will is no longer apparent does not revoke that part of the will if T had no intention to revoke. For example, if T accidentally spills ink on his will completely obliterating some words, these words are not deemed to have been revoked. Recourse may thus be had to any available means, natural or artificial as well as to extrinsic evidence, with a view to ascertaining the obliterated words (see *Townley v Watson* (1844)).

Conditional obliteration

If T's intention to partially revoke his will by obliterating certain words is conditional, revocation will not occur unless the relevant condition is fulfilled. For example, T may in his will make a legacy of £500 to B and later cross out the £500 completely and insert £1,000 above it, intending that the original legacy will be revoked only if the alteration is effective. If it is not effective for any reason, the original legacy will not be revoked even if the figure of £500 is totally obliterated and is no longer apparent. In such a case artificial devices as well as natural means may be employed to ascertain the obliterated words (see *In the Goods of Itter*).

Revival of wills

Where a will or codicil has been revoked, it may later be restored to effect through its *revival*. Under s 22 WA such revival may be by:

(i) re-execution; or

(ii)by a duly executed codicil.

Intention to revive

In the case of revival by means of a duly executed codicil, s 22 prescribes that the codicil must show an intention to revive the revoked will or codicil. The courts have tended to construe this requirement strictly. For example, in *Marsh v Marsh* (1860), taping a codicil to a revoked will was held not to suffice as evidence of an intention to revive the will.

The courts have also held in *In the Goods of Steele* (1868); *In the Goods of May* (1868) and *In the Goods of Wilson* (1868) that a revoked will is not revived by a subsequent codicil which merely refers to the will by date without any specific indication that it was intended to revive it.

By contrast, it was held in *Re Baker* that if the codicil not only referred to the revoked will by date but went further to refer to its provisions, this served as evidence of an intention to revive.

In addition, the courts may be able to discover an intention to revive not only from the codicil itself but also from extrinsic evidence. In *In the Goods of Davis* (1952), T made a will leaving his estate to EPH which was automatically revoked when they married the next year. Upon learning of the revocation, T wrote on the envelope containing the will: 'EPH is now my lawful wedded wife.' This was signed by T and two witnesses as required by s 9. This writing was held to be a codicil which the court deduced from the surrounding circumstances was intended to revive the will.

Revival where a will has been revoked in stages

Under s 22, if a will or codicil is partly revoked, then wholly revoked and is later revived, the part that was first revoked is not revived unless a contrary intention is shown. For example, if in 1993 T makes a will leaving his realty to A and his personalty to B; in 1994, T revokes the devise to A and in 1995 revokes the whole will, the devise will not be restored if the will is subsequently revived.

The position where a revoking will is itself revoked

Where an earlier will is revoked by a later will or codicil which is in turn revoked, this in itself does not revive the first will (see *In the Goods of Hodgkinson* (1893); *Major v Williams* (1843) and *In the Goods of Browne* (1858)).

No revival of will revoked by destruction

Revival is only possible where a revoked will still exists. In effect, a will that was revoked by destruction cannot be revived (see *Rogers v Goodenough* (1862) and *In the Goods of Steele* (1868)).

Republication of wills

While revival restores a revoked will to effect, *republication* confirms a valid will so that it takes effect as if made, not on the date it was executed but on the date it was republished.

As in the case of revival, a will or codicil may be republished either by re-execution or by a duly executed codicil.

With regard to republication by re-execution, the very fact that T re-executes his will, raises a rebuttable presumption that he intended to republish it (see *Dunn v Dunn* (1866)).

In the case of republication by codicil, evidence is required to show that T intended that the codicil would republish the will. For example, in *Re Smith* (1890) T 's codicil which made no reference to his earlier will was held not to have republished that will.

If T intends a codicil executed by him to republish his earlier will, it is usual for him to state this expressly in the codicil. Even if he does not, cases like *Skinner v Ogle* (1845); *Re Taylor* (1880); *Re Champion* (1893) and *Re Harvey* (1945) have held that once the codicil contains any reference to the will, T will be taken to have evinced an intention to republish the will.

Consequences of republication

By virtue of s 34 WA, a republished will is deemed to have been executed on the date of republication (see also *Goonerwardene v Goonerwardene* (1931)).

This has several far-reaching consequences as follows:

Unattested alterations

Where an alteration contained in a will was made after it was executed, but the alteration itself was not executed it will be rendered effective by republication of the will, provided there is evidence that it preceded the republication (see *In the Goods of Sykes* (1873)).

Incorporation by reference

As a general rule, only a document in existence when a will was executed may be incorporated by reference into the will (see *Singleton v Tomlinson* (1878)). Where a will is republished, a document prepared after its execution may be incorporated into it, if the document had come into being by the republication date (see *In the Goods of Truro* (1866)).

Gifts in favour of beneficiaries referred to by description

Where T in his will leaves property to A by name and A dies before T, the gift in A's favour will lapse even if the will is later republished (see *Hutcheson v Hammond* (1790) and *Re Woods Will* (1861)).

However, where the reference to the will is not to a named beneficiary but to one who is described by his relationship to T or some other person and the party fitting this description when the will was made dies, republication of the will operates to confer the benefit on any other person fitting the description at T's death (see *Re Hardyman* (1925)).

Gifts of property made by reference to the present time

By virtue of s 24 WA, a will speaks from T's death as regards both his realty and his personalty unless T employed words which show that a disposition was restricted to property owned by him at the date of the will, eg where T makes a devise of 'all the freehold property of which I am possessed at the date of this my will'.

Where a devise or bequest relates to property owned by T at the date of the will, the effect of republishing the will is that the gift will extend to any other property of that type acquired by T between the date the will was made and the republication date as seen from *Re Champion* and *Re Reeves* (1928).

Witnessing the will

Where a will was witnessed by a beneficiary or his spouse, s 15 WA provides that the benefit is thereby lost. However, if it is later republished and persons other than the beneficiary and his spouse witness the republication, the benefit will be restored (see *Anderson v Anderson* (1872) and *Re Trotter* (1899)).

Exercising powers of appointment

Where T exercises a power of appointment by will before he becomes entitled to do so, such an exercise may subsequently be validated by republishing the will after he has become so entitled.

4 The failure of gifts in a will

Classes of gifts in a will

A gift of personal property by means of a will is called a *legacy* or *bequest*; while a gift of real property is called a *devise*.

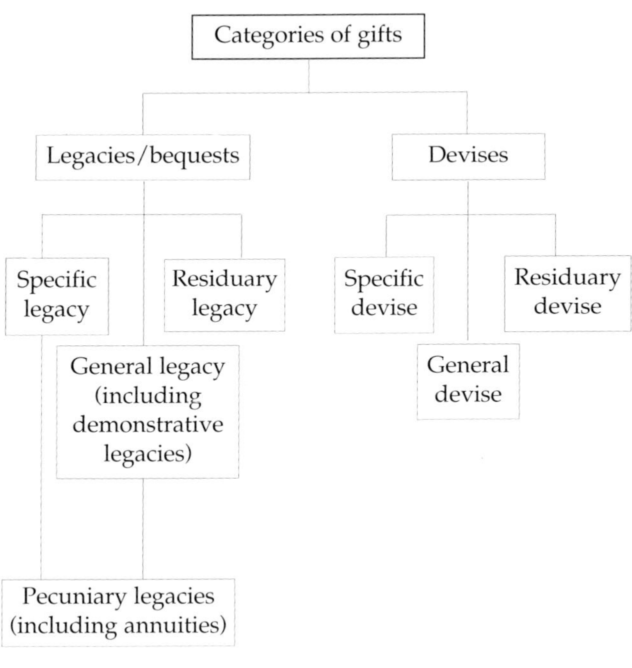

Types of legacies

Specific legacy

This is a gift of specified personal property forming part of T's estate at his death which is severed or distinguished from the totality of his assets (see *Bothamley v Sherson* (1875)).

An intention to make a specific legacy is usually manifested by:

- the use of 'my' or similar possessive words; eg 'my Ford Fiesta to A'; or 'all the watches I own to B'.
- referring to the manner in which the subject-matter of the gift was acquired. For example, 'I give to E the diamond ring my husband gave me on our 50th wedding anniversary'.

It has, however, been pointed out in *Re Rose* (1948) that the courts lean against specific legacies. This means in practice that, where it is not clear whether a legacy is specific or general, it is usually construed to be a general legacy (see, eg *Re Willcocks* (1921); *Re Gage* (1934) and *Re O'Connor* (1948)).

General legacy

This is a gift of personalty which is not a bequest of any specific part of T's estate but is intended to be provided for out of the general assets owned by T at his death. Unlike a specific legacy, the subject-matter of a general legacy need not form part of T's estate at his death. For example, if T in his will leaves to B '10 bottles of 1920 vintage port' or '500 ICI shares' (as distinct from 'the 10 bottles of 1920 vintage port in my wine cellar' or 'the 500 ICI shares owned by me'), this is a general legacy. If T does not own the 10 bottles of port or the shares at his death, it is incumbent on his executors to use funds from his estate to purchase them for B (see *Bothamley v Sherson*).

Where the subject-matter of a general legacy is *money* this is also called a *pecuniary legacy*. For example, 'I hereby leave £1,000 to B'. But *note* that a gift of money by will may also be a specific rather than a general legacy. For example, a gift of 'the money in my wallet/safe to B' (see *Lawson v Stitch* (1738)).

Demonstrative legacy

This is a legacy which is intended to be satisfied primarily out of a specified fund or specified part of T's estate. As Lord Thurlow LC explained in *Ashburner v MacGuire* (1786), it is 'in its nature a general legacy but where a particular fund is pointed out to satisfy it'. For example, '£900 to B out of my current account with the Bank of Wales'; or '£3,000 to B to be paid to him out of my partnership share' (see *Re Webster* (1945)).

Note, however, that where a will directs that a legacy should be paid *exclusively* (rather than *primarily*) out of a specified fund, it will be a specific and not a demonstrative legacy (see *Paget v Huish* (1863)).

Annuities

An annuity under a will is a legacy of money payable by instalments. Each instalment is treated as a separate legacy, and thus an annuity, as Cross J declared in *Re Earl of Berkeley* is to all intents and purposes 'a series of legacies payable at intervals'. In common with other legacies, annuities may be specific, general or demonstrative.

Residuary legacy

This is a legacy or bequest of T's personal property remaining after all his debts, liabilities, expenses and other legacies have been satisfied.

Types of devises

A devise of realty under a will may be a specific devise which has as its subject-matter, specific property which forms part of the testator's estate and which is severed or distinguished from the general mass of his estate. For example, 'I give to B in fee simple my dwelling house at 100 Mount Pleasant Drive, Swansea'.

A will may also include one or more *general devises*. For example, 'I hereby direct my executors to purchase for B, a holiday cottage in the Gower'.

Finally, it is quite common for a will to contain a *residuary devise*. For example, 'I hereby devise to B all my real property not otherwise disposed of by this will'.

Failure of gifts in a will

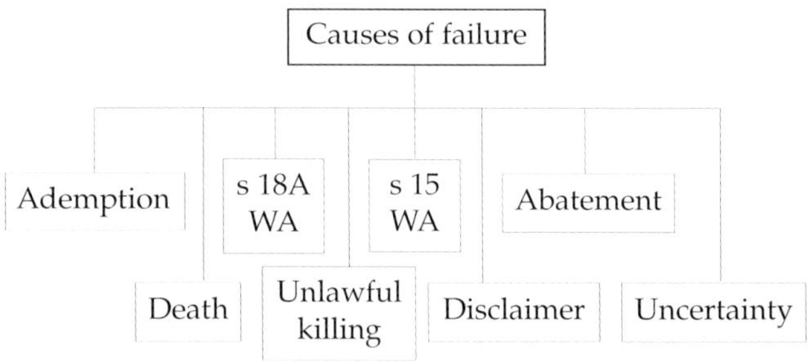

Ademption

Where T has made a *specific* legacy or devise but at his death the property no longer exists/belongs to him or has been converted into other property, the gift is adeemed. Under the doctrine of ademption, the intended beneficiary loses his entitlement. Ademption occurs in a variety of contexts, eg where:

- T bequeaths 'my 200 BT shares to B' and later sells all the shares (total ademption) or some of them (partial ademption) (see *Harris v Jackson* (1877) and *Ashburner v Macguire*). B cannot claim the purchase price and if T thereafter purchases other shares in the same company, the gift is not revived (see *Re Gibson* (1866)).

- T bequeaths 'my engagement ring to B' and the ring is stolen. B not only loses his entitlement but cannot claim any insurance money paid in respect of the loss (see *Durant v Friend*).

- T bequeaths the £1,000 which X owes him to B. If X repays this sum in T's lifetime, B's interest in the £1,000 is adeemed (see *Re Bridle* (1879) and *Aston v Wood* (1874)).

- T devises his dwelling house to B but the house is repossessed or later sold by T as was the case in *Re Bagot's Settlement* (1862).

- T includes in his will an annuity in B's favour charged upon and exclusively payable out of specific property and the property is later disposed of by T (see *Cowper v Mantell* (1856)).

- T devises his dwelling house to B and later enters into a *specifically enforceable contract* to sell the house to Z, but dies before completion. In such an event, there is a notional conversion of the dwelling house into personalty which operates to adeem the gift to B (see *Farrar v Earl of Winterton* (1842); *Watts v Watts* (1873); *Re Edwards* (1958) and *Re Sweeting* (1988)).

  Note, however, that if the contract of sale was made *before* the will is executed there will be no ademption and B can therefore claim the purchase price (see *Re Callow* (1928)).

- T makes a specific gift of property to B and later confers on Z an option to purchase the property which Z exercises after T's death. The effect of the rule in *Lawes v Bennet* is that the gift to B will be adeemed (see *Re Carrington* (1932)).

By contrast, if T granted the option before executing the will, there will be no ademption (see *Drant v Vause* (1842) and *Weeding v Weeding* (1859)).

Position where property changes in form but not in substance

Ademption will not occur where T makes a gift of specific property and the property has since the making of the will changed in name or in form but the substance remains the same (see *Re Clifford* (1912); *Re Leeming* (1912) and *Re Dorman* (1994)). But contrast these cases with *Re Slater* (1907).

Effect of republication on ademption

An adeemed gift is not re-instated by republishing a will. For example, if T makes a specific gift of 1,000 British Airways shares to B and later sells the shares and invests the proceeds in 1,000 ICI shares, republication of the will at a still later date does not revive the adeemed gift so as to entitle B to the ICI shares at T's death (see *Drinkwater v Falconer* (1755); *Powys v Mansfield* and *Re Galway's WT* (1950)).

Exceptionally, however, republication may alter the construction of a will in such a manner that a specific gift will be saved from ademption as was the case in *Re Reeves* (1928). T made a will in 1921 in which he gave B 'all my interest in my *present lease*'. The only lease held by T at the date of the will expired in 1924 and T took out a new lease of the property. Some time later, T republished his 1921 will. It was held that this gift would ordinarily have been adeemed in 1924 when the initial lease expired but that the effect of republication was that the phrase 'my present lease' referred to the new lease and this saved the gift from ademption. Since the new lease was still in force when T died, B was accordingly entitled to it.

Avoiding ademption by express provisions in the will

T can prevent the ademption of a specific gift by inserting an appropriate clause into his will, eg 'I hereby bequeath to B, my 500 British Gas shares *or the investments or assets representing the same at my death, if they shall have been converted into other holdings*' (see *Re Lewis's WT* (1937)).

No ademption of general and demonstrative legacies

Neither a general nor a demonstrative gift will fail by ademption in the same way as a specific one. Thus, if T's will reads 'I hereby leave 500 shares in XYZ Ltd to B' and T owns no such shares on his death, his executors must have recourse to his assets to give effect to this legacy (see *Bothamley v Sherson*).

The death of a beneficiary

The general rule

A gift in a will lapses if the intended beneficiary dies before T (see *Elliot v Davenport* (1905) and *Maybank v Brooks* (1780)).

A provision in a will expressly excluding the doctrine of lapse will be ineffective (see *Re Ladd* (1932)). T may, however, prevent a gift from lapsing by inserting in a gift to B, a proviso that if B dies before T, the property is to pass on T's death to B's personal representatives to be part of B's estate (see *Sibley v Cook* (1747) and *Re Cousens WT* (1937)).

Gifts to co-owners

Where T leaves property to B1 and B2 as *tenants in common* and B1 dies before T, his share lapses (see *Page v Page* (1728); *Peat v Chapman* (1750) and *Re Wood* (1861)). Where the property is left to them as *joint tenants* and B1 dies before T, the whole property goes to B2 (see *Morley v Bird* (1798)).

Class gifts

A gift to a specified class to be ascertained when T dies will not lapse if a member of the class dies before T (see *Stewart v Sheffield* (1811); *Shuttleworth v Greaves* (1838) and *Shaw v M'Mahon* (1842)).

Effect of republication

Where B, a named beneficiary, dies before T, republication of T's will after B dies does not prevent lapse (see *Hutcheson v Hammond* (1790) and *Re Wood*).

On the other hand, if the intended beneficiary is described rather than named and B who fitted the description when the will was made dies in T's lifetime, republication entitles any other person who fits the description at T's death to take the gift (see *Re Hardyman* (1925)).

Uncertainty as to the order of death

In cases where the order of death as between T and B is uncertain, the *commorientes* rule in s 184 LPA comes into operation. Under this rule, the older of the two is presumed to have died first (see *Hickman v Peacey* (1945); *Re Pringle* (1946); *Re Bate* (1947) *Re Whitrick* (1957) and *Re Rowland* (1963)).

T may, however, circumvent the operation of this presumption, if he wishes, by inserting in his will a *commorientes* clause which expressly provides that the gift to B will take effect only if B outlives T by a specified period (usually 28 days).

Exclusion of the doctrine of lapse by s 33 WA

It is provided in s 33 WA (as amended by s 19 AJA) that where T makes a gift by will to B who is his child or remoter descendant, and B dies before T, the gift will not lapse, if:

- B was survived by issue at his death; and
- B had issue living at T's death.

Note, s 33 applies even if B's issue living at T's death is not the same person as the issue who survived B at his death (see *In the Goods of Parker* (1860)).

The original s 33 which applies in cases where T died before 1983 differs in several notable respects from the amended s 33 (which applies where T's death is after 1982). In particular:

- It was expressly provided in the original s 33 that a gift would be saved from lapsing only where its subject-matter consisted of an estate or interest which was not determinable at or before B's death (see *Re Butler* (1918) and *Re Wilson* (1939)).

This restriction has, however, been omitted from the amended s 33.

- The *original s 33* applied only if B had issue living at T's death (see *Elliot v Joicey* (1935)). For its part, the amended s 33 applies where, although B has no issue living at T's death, he does have issue *en ventre sa mère* (ie in its mother's womb) provided such issue is eventually born alive.
- Under the *original s 33*, where a gift was saved from lapsing, the property affected became part of B's estate. This meant, eg:
  - that if B made a will leaving his entire estate to his mistress, the property would pass to her and not to

his issue whose existence had saved the gift from lapsing;

- that if B's estate when originally administered was insufficient to pay his creditors, the property would instead of passing to his issue, be used for this purpose (see *Re Basioli* (1953); *Re Pearson* (1920); *Johnson v Johnson* (1843) and *Re Hayter* (1937)).

By contrast, the *amended* s 33 provides that the property in question will pass directly to B's issue.

- the *original* s 33 did not apply where T left property to his children/remoter descendants as a *class* to be ascertained at T's death. For example, if T who had three children (C1, C2 and C3) left £30,000 'to all my children' in his will and C1 died before T but left issue who were still living at T's death, the £30,000 would pass to C2 and C3 to the exclusion of C1's issue.

The *amended* s 33 provides that in such circumstances, the share which C1 would have received if he had survived T (ie £10,000) will pass to his issue.

Failure on divorce or annulment of marriage

Where T is married to B and leaves property to B in his or her will but the marriage is later dissolved or annulled, s 18A WA provides that the gift lapses unless there is a contrary intention in the will. *Note*, however, that this provision applies only in cases where T's death occurs after 1982.

Where the interest conferred on B by the gift is a life interest, such a lapse accelerates the interest of the remainderman.

Where the gift was intended to confer an absolute interest on B, the effect of the lapse is that the property concerned passes to whoever is entitled to T's residue.

A difficulty has, however, arisen where the property in question is given to B absolutely but is accompanied by a substitutional gift to X if B died before T. A gift of this nature fell to be considered in *Re Sinclair* (1985) where it was held that insofar as B was still alive when T died, the substitutional gift would fail in spite of the lapse of the primary gift to B.

This was considered unsatisfactory and Parliament has intervened by enacting s 3 Law Reform (Succession) Act 1995. The effect of s 3 is that where T dies after 1995, the substitutional gift in favour of X will be valid, notwithstanding the fact that T's former spouse, B, is still alive.

Forfeiture of benefit through unlawful killing

> There is a long-standing and well-established rule of public policy known as the forfeiture rule which precludes a person who has unlawfully killed another from acquiring a benefit in consequence of the killing – *per* Judge Kolbert in *Jones v Roberts* (1994).

In accordance with this policy, it was decided in *In the Estate of Crippen* (1911) that B would lose his entitlement to any benefit under T's will, if he was convicted of T's murder.

By the same token, it has been held in cases like *In the Estate of Hall* (1914); *Re Giles* (1972) and *Royse v Royse* (1985) that if B is convicted of the manslaughter of T, he is liable to forfeit any benefits due to him under T's will.

In *Re H (Deceased)* (1990), Peter Gibson J laid down the requirement that manslaughter would result in forfeiture only if B had been guilty of 'deliberate, intentional and unlawful violence or threats thereof'. This decision has, however, been called into question in *Jones v Roberts*, on the ground that it was inconsistent with the more authoritative decision of the Court of Appeal in *Royse* which was not referred to in *Re H (Deceased).*

The application of the forfeiture rule is subject to certain qualifications:

- Forfeiture will not occur where B, in killing T, was insane to such a degree that he was unable to understand the nature and quality of his acts or comprehend that what he was doing was wrong (see *Re Houghton* (1915); *Re Pitts* (1931) and *Jones v Roberts*).
- The forfeiture rule is not stringently applied where B's conviction for manslaughter resulted from a motor accident (see *Jones v Roberts*).
- The Forfeiture Act (1982) provides that where B is precluded by the forfeiture rule from acquiring any interest in T's estate, he may apply to the court for relief against forfeiture except in cases where he has been convicted of T's murder.

Where an application is made, the court may modify the forfeiture rule by making any order which will meet the justice of the case, having regard to the conduct of B and T respectively as well as other material circumstances.

Cases in which relief against forfeiture has been granted include:

- *Re K (Deceased)* (1985): where B, who had endured years of violence at the hands of her husband T, pointed a gun at him during a violent quarrel and he was killed when it went off;
- *Re H (Deceased)* (1990): where B had killed his wife T while in a state of deep depression brought on by the mistaken belief that she was having an affair and was

convicted of manslaughter with a finding of diminished responsibility on T's part; and

- *Re S (Deceased)* (1996): where B, who was the chief beneficiary under an life insurance policy taken out by his wife and who had killed her because he suspected she was having an affair, applied for his entitlement under the policy to pass to his infant son.

Failure where beneficiary or spouse is a witness

Section 15 WA contemplates that where T's will is witnessed either by B or by B's spouse, this causes the gift in B's favour to lapse.

As explained by Russell LJ in *Re Bravda* (1968), s 15 is intended 'to ensure reliable, unbiased witness of due execution'. In this case, T executed a home-made will leaving his estate to his daughters, B1 and B2. The will was witnessed by W1 and W2. As an afterthought, T asked B1 and B2 who were also present to sign and it was held that by signing they had lost their entitlement.

Exceptions to s 15

The act of witnessing a will does not cause a gift to lapse in the following contexts:

- Under s 1 WA 1968 (which applies only in cases where T dies after 29 May 1969), the attestation of a will by B or B's spouse is superfluous and of no effect if it would be duly executed without this attestation. This means, in effect, that once there are at least two attesting witnesses other than B or his spouse, s 15 no longer operates to deprive B of his entitlement (as happened for instance in *Re Bravda* where T died before this Act came into force).

- Where a will is privileged, it need not be witnessed. It has consequently been held in *Re Limond* (1915) that the fact that B has witnessed a privileged will, does not deprive him of his benefit thereunder.

- Where a will has been witnessed by B's spouse but its execution occurred before they got married, it has been established in *Thorpe v Bestwick* (1881) that the gift to B will not lapse.

- Where a person to whom property is left in a will, receives it as a trustee rather than a beneficiary, the fact that the will has been witnessed by that person or his spouse does not cause the gift to lapse; as seen from cases like *Cresswell v Cresswell* (1868) and *Re Ray's WT* (1936).

- Where B or his spouse does not witness the will in which property is left to him, but a codicil thereto, it emerges from *Re Marcus* (1887) that the gift to B will not lapse.

- Where the original will was witnessed by B or his spouse and was later republished by a codicil witnessed by other persons, the republication has the effect of saving the gift from lapsing (see *Anderson v Anderson* (1872) and *Re Trotter* (1899)).

- Where a secret trust is created in B's favour and the property is transferred to the intended trustee by means of a will, it has been held in *Re Young* (1951) that the fact that B witnessed the will does not deprive him of entitlement under the trust.

Disclaimer

Where property is left to B in a will, he is entitled to reject the gift since 'the law is certainly not so absurd as to force a person to take an estate against his will'. Such a rejection by

B is called a disclaimer. A disclaimer may be by deed, in writing or by conduct.

B's entitlement to disclaim is subject to certain qualifications:

- There can be no disclaimer once B has accepted the gift (see *Re Hodge* (1940)).
- Where a single gift consists of several distinct assets, B must either accept or disclaim the whole gift (see *Guthrie v Walrond* (1882) and *Re Joel* (1943)).
- Where a gift is to B1 and B2 as joint tenants, a disclaimer will be effective only if it is made by both of them. If B1 wishes to disclaim while B2 wishes to accept, the most that can be done is for B1 to release his interest in the property to B2 (see *Re Schar* (1951)).
- After disclaiming, B may revive his entitlement under the will by retracting his disclaimer. Retraction will not, however, be permitted where some other party has altered his position on the strength of the disclaimer (see *Re Cranstoun's WT* (1949)).

Failure by abatement

Where an asset which has been bequeathed or devised to B is required to discharge T's expenses, debts and liabilities in accordance with the order of payment laid down in Part II, First Schedule to the AEA, this causes the bequest or devise to abate. The effect of this is that B loses his entitlement under the will either completely or to the extent that the property which was left to him is required to pay such expenses, debts etc (see further Chapter 7 pp 135–39).

Failure due to uncertainty

Uncertainty as to subject-matter

A gift in a will is liable to fail if the subject-matter of the gift is not identified with sufficient certainty. In *Asten v Asten* (1894), T made separate devises to each of his four sons of 'all that newly built house, being No.   Sudeley Place'. Although T owned four houses in Sudeley Place, the devises failed for uncertainty of subject-matter since the will did not indicate the precise house which was to pass to each son. See also *Peck v Halsey* (1726), where the words employed were 'some of my best linen'; and *Jubber v Jubber* (1839) where the material words were 'a handsome gratuity'.

Uncertainty as to beneficiaries

Where a gift in a will is framed in terms that make it impossible to determine the intended beneficiaries, such a gift is liable to fail. In *Re Stephenson* (1897), T had an aunt (his father's sister). She had three sons who bore the surname Bamber. When making his will, T knew that the sons had all died, each leaving children. T nevertheless left his residuary estate 'unto the children of the deceased son (named Bamber) of my father's sister'. The gift failed because it was impossible to tell which of the three sons was being referred to.

Effect of the failure of a gift

Specific gifts

Where a *specific bequest* of personalty fails and its subject-matter is still available for distribution it generally passes to T's residuary legatee (see *Leake v Robinson* (1817); *Cambridge v Rous* (1802); and *Re Backhouse* (1931)).

Equally, where a *specific devise* of real property fails and the property is still available for distribution, it will generally pass to T's residuary devisee (see s 25 WA and *Re Mason* (1901)).

Residuary gifts

Where a gift of residuary personalty or realty fails in its entirety, the property concerned will devolve on those persons who would be entitled to the testator's estate if he died intestate.

Again, if the residuary estate is left to B1 and B2 in undivided shares and the gift to B1 fails, his share of the residue will not ordinarily pass to B2, but to those entitled on intestacy.

Acceleration

The doctrine of acceleration applies in cases where successive interests are created in the same property. For example, where T in his will devises Blackacre to B1 for life remainder to B2 absolutely. If the gift to B1 fails, the effect of the doctrine as seen from cases like *Jull v Jacobs* (1876) and *Re Hodge* (1943) is that the remainder in B2's favour takes effect in possession on T's death.

However, if the remainder is expressed to be contingent (eg 'to B1 for life remainder to B2 if he attains the age of 21') and B1's prior life interest fails, there will be no acceleration until the contingency is fulfilled (see *Re Townsend* (1886)).

5 Intestate succession

Introduction

Intestacy occurs where a person dies without effectively disposing of his property by will. Intestacy may be total or partial.

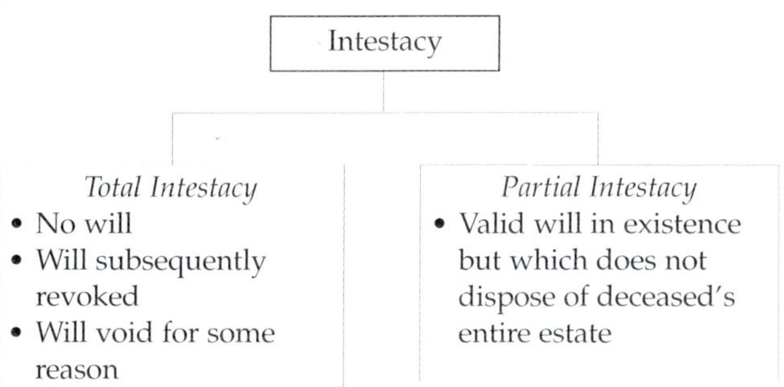

Where a person dies intestate, his estate must be administered and distributed by his personal representative (pr) in accordance with the provisions of the AEA 1925 as amended by later Acts such as the Intestates' Estate Act 1952, the Family Provision Act 1966 and the Family Law Reform Acts 1969 and 1987.

Far-reaching amendments were proposed in the Law Commission Report, *'Distribution on Intestacy'* (1989), most notably the proposal that the whole estate of an intestate who was survived by a spouse should in all circumstances pass to the spouse. While rejecting this proposal, the government accepted other recommendations put forward in the report which are now embodied in the Law (Reform)

Succession Act 1995. By virtue of this Act, the rules governing the distribution of the estate of persons dying intestate after 31 December 1995, now differ in several material respects from the rules which had hitherto applied.

Administration of the deceased's property pending distribution

Section 33 AEA prescribes the manner in which prs are to deal with the property of an intestate prior to its distribution.

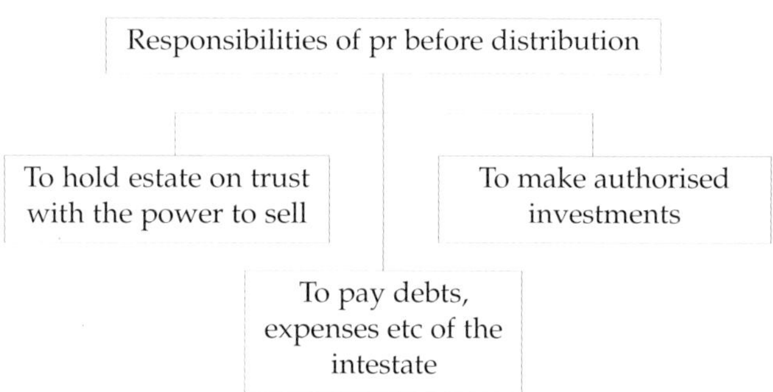

The Statutory Trust for Sale (s 33(1))

The pr is required to hold the deceased's real property and his personal property not consisting of money on trust. Under the original s 33, these assets were required to be held on trust for sale with a power to postpone sale. However, with the abolition of trusts for sale by the Trusts of Land and Appointment of Trustees Act (1996), s 33(1) has now been amended to provide that the prs of a person who died intestate are to hold his estate on trust with a power to postpone sale.

Payment of debts, expenses etc (s 33(2))

The pr must pay any funeral/administration expenses, debts and liabilities of the deceased. He may, for this purpose, use any ready money available and the net money arising from selling the deceased's assets.

The power to invest (s 33(3))

Before distribution occurs, and in particular, during the minority of a beneficiary or subsistence of a life interest in the estate, the pr is empowered to invest the proceeds realised from the sale of property not yet distributed in investments authorised by statute.

Total intestacy

After payment of the intestate's expenses, debts and other liabilities, his residuary estate becomes available for distribution in the manner provided in s 46 AEA.

The residuary estate consists of any money left in a pr's hands and any investments acquired with such money, together with any part of the intestate's estate that has been retained unsold and is not required for administration purposes (see s 33(4) AEA).

Devolution on intestacy under s 46 AEA

Category of beneficiaries	Entitlement
• *Surviving spouse* ○ Where intestate has no surviving issue/ relatives in the specified categories:	Surviving spouse takes entire residuary estate.
○ Where intestate is also survived by issue:	Surviving spouse takes: – personal chattels; – statutory legacy; – life interest in half of the remaining residuary estate.
○ Where intestate has no surviving issue but is survived by relatives in the specified categories:	Surviving spouse takes: – personal chattels; – statutory legacy (higher amount); – absolute interest in half of remaining residuary estate.
• *Issue of intestate* ○ Where intestate has no surviving spouse:	Entire residuary estate held on statutory trusts for issue (s 47 AEA).
○ Where intestate is also survived by spouse:	– half of residuary estate after spouse gets personal chattels/statutory legacy is held on statutory trust for issue; – the issue are also entitled to the other half on the death of the spouse.

• *Other relatives of intestate* ❍ Where intestate has no surviving issue but is survived by spouse and relatives in the specified categories (ie parents, brothers or sisters of the whole blood or their issue):	These relatives are entitled to half the estate remaining after the spouse has taken personal chattels/ statutory legacy.
❍ Where intestate is not survived by spouse or issue:	His relatives are entitled as follows: – parents; – brothers/sisters of the whole blood; – brothers/sisters of the half blood; – grandparents; – uncles/aunts of the whole blood; – uncles/aunts of the half blood.
❍ Where there are no relatives:	The estate passes to the Crown as *bona vacantia.*

The position of the surviving spouse

Where a person dies intestate survived by a spouse, that spouse is usually the chief beneficiary under the intestacy rules.

Where both spouses died in circumstances which make it impossible to determine which one died first and the older of the two died intestate, the presumption in s 184 LPA that death occurred in order of seniority is excluded by s 46(3) AEA. This means in effect that under the intestacy rules, the younger spouse is not deemed to have survived the older one.

It is further provided by the Law Reform (Succession) Act 1995 that if a person dies intestate after December 1995 and is outlived by his or her spouse by no more than 28 days, the spouse will be deemed not to have survived the intestate.

The extent of the entitlement of the surviving spouse: For the purpose of determining the precise entitlement of a surviving spouse, it must be ascertained whether the intestate:

- was also survived by issue; or
- was also was survived by his parent(s), brother(s) or sister(s) of the whole blood or any issue of such brother/sister.

Where there are no surviving relatives in these categories

The surviving spouse of the intestate is entitled to the entire residuary estate.

Where there are issue in addition to the surviving spouse

Provided any such issue attains the age of 18 or marries before that age, the entitlement of the surviving spouse is restricted to:

(i) *An absolute interest in the intestates personal chattels*: According to s 55(1)(x) AEA, personal chattels include:

  - carriages, horses, stable furniture etc;
  - motor cars and accessories;
  - garden effects;

- domestic animals;
- plate, plated articles, linen, china and glass;
- books, pictures and prints;
- furniture, ornaments or articles of household or personal use;
- jewellery;
- musical instruments;
- scientific instruments and apparatus; and
- wines, liquors and other consumables.

Items which the courts have held to be personal chattels include:

Case	Description of item
Re Chaplin (1950)	Yacht used for leisure sailing.
Re Macculough (1981)	But not one used for business.
Re Reynolds (1966)	Stamp collection assembled as a hobby.
Re Crispin (1975)	Collection of clocks and watches.
Re Collins (1971)	Collection of valuable bank notes/ coins.
Re Hutchison (1955)	Racehorses kept for recreation.
Re Ogilby (1942)	But not cattle bred as farm stock.

(ii) *The statutory legacy*: This is a pecuniary legacy paid to the surviving spouse. The sum payable depends on when the intestate died and is as follows:

Period of death	Sum payable as statutory legacy
March 1977 – 28 February 1981	£25,000
1 March 1981 – 31 May 1987	£40,000
1 June 1987 – 30 November 1998	£75,000
1 December 1993 to date	£125,000

(iii) *An interest in the residue*: The surviving spouse is also entitled to a *life interest* in *one-half* of whatever is left of the residuary estate after the personal chattels and the statutory legacy have been set aside, while the other half will be held on trust for the issue of the intestate.

Under s 47A(1) AEA, a surviving spouse may elect to redeem the life interest and receive its capital value. This must be done in writing within 12 months of the grant of administration.

Where the intestate is not survived by issue but is survived by some other relatives in the above categories

The surviving spouse will be entitled to:

- the personal chattels;
- a statutory legacy of *£125,000* if the intestate died before 30 November, 1993 and *£200,000* if he or she dies after that date;
- an absolute interest in half of what is left of the residuary estate. The other half devolves on the relatives of the intestate in the following order:
    - the intestate's parent(s) if still living. If not then;

- the intestate's surviving brother's and sisters, if any. If there are none then;
- any surviving issue of the intestate's brothers or sisters of the whole blood.

The spouses right to appropriate the matrimonial home

Section 41 AEA empowers a pr to appropriate any asset owned by the deceased in or towards satisfying any interest in his estate. For example, if H owned a dwelling house in which he lived with his wife, W, until his death intestate, the pr could by virtue of s 41 allow W to retain the house in satisfaction of her statutory legacy.

The problem with s 41 in this context, was that unless the pr was prepared to exercise his power of appropriation, a surviving spouse had no right to retain the matrimonial home. This problem has now been resolved by s 5 Intestates' Estates Act 1952 which gives the surviving spouse a right to require the pr to exercise his power of appropriation with regard to the matrimonial home.

This must be done by giving notice in writing to the prs within 12 months of the grant of administration to them. During this period, the pr cannot sell or otherwise dispose of the property concerned unless this is necessary for administration purposes.

The right of a surviving spouse exists whether the deceased was a freeholder or leaseholder except where the deceased held a tenancy that was determinable within two years of his death.

The right of the surviving spouse can only be exercised with the court's consent in four situations, namely, where the property:

- is part of a larger building and the interest in the whole building falls within the deceased's residuary estate;
- forms part of agricultural land falling within the estate;
- was in use as a hotel/boarding house at the intestate's death;
- was used in part for some non-domestic purpose.

Under s 41 AEA, appropriation is possible only if the value of the appropriated asset is *less than* or *equal to* the interest of the beneficiary to whom it is appropriated. By contrast, the right to require appropriation under the 1952 Act avails a surviving spouse whether the value of the matrimonial home is less than, equal to, or exceeds the value of their entitlement under the intestacy rules. Where the value of the matrimonial home is greater, he or she must, however, make good the difference (see *Re Phelps* (1979)).

The entitlement of the issue

- *Where there is also a surviving spouse:* After the surviving spouse has taken the personal chattels and statutory legacy, the remaining estate is held on *statutory trusts*. Under these trusts:
    - one-half of the estate is held on trust for the spouse for life remainder to the issue; and
    - the other half is held on trust for the issue.
- *Where there are issue but no surviving spouse:* The whole estate of the intestate will be held on statutory trusts for them.

The substance of the statutory trust

Section 47(1) AEA provides that where the residuary estate

or any part of it is held on statutory trusts for the issue of the intestate. This means in effect that:

- children of the intestate living at his death (including any child who is *en ventre sa mère*) will be entitled in equal shares;
- if a child of the intestate predeceased him, the issue of the deceased child living at the death of the intestate (including any child who is *en ventre sa mère*) will be entitled in equal shares to whatever share their parent would have received if he or she had been alive at the intestate's death;
- no child or other issue of the intestate becomes entitled to a vested interest in his or her share until (s)he attains the age of 18 or marries under that age.

The hotchpot rule (s 47(1)(iii) AEA)

The rule requires certain benefits conferred by the intestate during his lifetime on his child to be brought into account in determining what share that child or their issue will be entitled under the statutory trusts. By virtue of the Law Reform (Succession) Act 1995, it applies only in respect of estates of persons dying before January 1996.

Even if the intestate died before 1996, the rule will not apply:

- where the intestate in conferring a benefit on one child expressed an intention to prefer that child to the others; or
- where such an intention can be inferred from the circumstances surrounding the gift.

Benefits brought into account

The hotchpot rule extends to money or property paid or settled by the intestate to/for the benefit of his child by way of advancement or on the child's marriage.

A payment or gift to a child which appears to be in the nature of a permanent provision is *prima facie* to be brought into account; eg purchase of house; transfer of shares (see *Hardy v Shaw* (1976)); or payment of lump sum to enable a child, to enter a profession or business (see *Taylor v Taylor* (1875)).

On the other hand, periodic payments made for the maintenance or education of the child or to provide temporary assistance will not ordinarily be brought into account under the hotchpot rule.

Remoter issue of the intestate

It is only those benefits which are conferred on a child of the intestate that are brought into account. This means, for instance, that if the intestate made a lifetime gift to his grandchild, this will not be taken into account in determining the share to be taken by the child of the intestate who is the parent of the grandchild. This is the case even where the parent of that grandchild dies before the intestate thereby causing his share to pass to that grandchild.

Value of the benefit

The value of benefits to be brought into account is assessed as at the intestate's death (see *Hardy v Shaw*).

Illustration of the hotchpot rule

Let us assume that Ann, a widow, has died intestate leaving a net residuary estate worth £140,000, and is survived by two adult sons Bert and Chris and two grandchildren Greg and Gail, who are the children of Ann's deceased daughter Daphne. During her lifetime, Ann purchased shares for Bert for which she paid £20,000 and at her death the shares were worth £40,000. She also gave £20,000 to Chris, £10,000 to Daphne and £5,000 to Greg at various stages.

Under the hotchpot rule, her estate will be distributed as follows:			
1 *Net residuary estate available for distribution*:			£140,000
2 *Benefits to be taken into account*: £40,000 (Bert's shares) + £20,000 (payment to Chris) + £10,000 (Payment to Daphne) =			£70,000
3 *Hotchpot pool to be divided* (1 + 2)			£210,000
4 *Entitlement of issue*:	Bert	Chris	Daphne's estate
3 of £210,000	£70,000	£70,000	£70,000
Minus benefits	£40,000	£20,000	£10,000
Amounts payable out of net estate	£30,000	£50,000 = **£140,000**	£60,000

Greg and Gail will each be entitled to £30,000 on statutory trusts, subject to attaining the age of 18 or getting married before then. As seen above, Greg as a grandchild does not have to bring into account the £5,000 given to him in Ann's lifetime.

The status of illegitimate and adopted children

Illegitimate children

At common law, an illegitimate child had no succession rights on the death intestate of either parent, his collaterals or remoter relatives.

When the AEA was first enacted in 1925, it did not alter the common law position. The first notable change was embodied in s 9 Legitimacy Act 1926 which provided for an illegitimate child to succeed to its mother's estate if she died intestate.

Further advances were made in s 14 Family Law Reform Act (FLRA) 1969. The effect of this statutory provision is that:

- an illegitimate child whose parent died intestate after 1969 would be entitled to succeed to his or her estate on the same footing as legitimate children;
- if an illegitimate child died before the parent survived by legitimate issue, such issue would succeed to the illegitimate child's entitlement;
- if an illegitimate child died intestate without issue, his parent(s), if alive, are entitled to succeed to his estate.

Note, however, that:

- the 1969 Act did entitle an illegitimate child to succeed on the death intestate of his other relatives;
- while an illegitimate child's legitimate offspring could under the Act succeed to the estate of a grandparent who died intestate, the illegitimate offspring of a legitimate child could not.

The changes in the 1969 Act were not considered to have gone far enough and so in 1987, another FLRA was enacted, which applies in the case of deaths occurring after 3 April 1988. The combined effect of ss 1 and 18 of this Act is that references to any relationship between two persons are to be considered without regard to whether the father and mother of either of them or of any persons through whom the relationship is deduced were married to each other at any time. In effect, where a person dies intestate after 3 April 1983, any entitlement to his or her estate will be determined without regard to whether any person in the line of succession is illegitimate.

The position of children born through artificial insemination
Where a child is born as a result of artificial insemination by a donor (AID) and the donor is not the mother's husband, the FLRA 1969, provided that if the identity of the father (ie the donor) was known, the child would in the event of intestacy be in the same position as any other child of that donor.

The position has been altered by the FLRA 1987 which provides that in the case of a child born by AID after 3 April 1988 to a married woman, whose husband was not the donor, the child is presumed to have been fathered by her husband unless he did not consent to the AID. This means that if he dies intestate, the child will have the same entitlements as his other children.

Adopted children
Where a child is adopted under an adoption order made in England or Wales or is adopted elsewhere and the adoption is recognised under English law, the Adoption Act 1976 provides that for purposes of intestacy, it is to be treated as the legitimate child of the adopter rather than its natural parents.

The entitlement of their relatives of the intestate
No other relatives of the intestate will be entitled under the intestacy rules where the intestate is survived by issue.

Where the intestate is survived by a spouse but no issue, as was seen above, the spouse is entitled to the personal chattels, a statutory legacy and half of the remaining estate absolutely; while the other half goes to specified relatives.

Where the intestate was not survived by a spouse or any issue, his residuary estate will be held on statutory trusts for his other relatives in the following order set out in s 46(1):

- the parents of the intestate in equal shares or whichever one of the two survived the deceased;
- brothers and sisters of the whole blood in equal shares;
- brothers and sisters of the half blood in equal shares;
- the grandparents of the intestate in equal shares or whichever one survives the intestate;
- the intestate's uncles/aunts of the whole blood in equal shares;
- the intestate's uncles/aunts of the half blood in equal shares.

Where there are no relatives in any of the above categories, the Crown takes the estate as *bona vacantia* but may make provision out of the estate for the intestate's dependants or any other persons for whom he might reasonably be expected to provide.

Partial intestacy

Partial intestacy may occur for a variety of reasons, for example:

- the will was incomplete or did not dispose of the residue;
- the residuary legatee/devisee died before the testator;
- the residuary gift was declared ineffective for some reason;
- the will was partially revoked.

The statutory trust for sale

Where a person dies partially intestate, the prs are required by s 33(1) AEA to hold that part of his estate not disposed of by his will under a statutory trust with an accompanying power of sale.

Payment of expenses, debts etc

Where partial intestacy occurs, s 33(2) contemplates that the pr must, in addition to paying the deceased's expenses, debts and liabilities, also set aside a sufficient sum to provide for any pecuniary legacies in the will.

Order of distribution on partial intestacy

In the event of partial intestacy, priority is accorded to the provisions of the will over the intestacy rules. This is confirmed by s 49(1) AEA which provides that Part IV AEA (including ss 46 and 47 which deal with distribution on intestacy) applies only to the part of the deceased's estate not disposed of by his will.

The hotchpot rules

These also apply in cases of partial intestacy where the deceased died before January 1996. In this connection, s 49(1) requires certain benefits given by such a deceased in his will to his or her surviving spouse or issue to be taken into account in determining what they will be entitled to under the intestacy rules.

The surviving spouse

Any beneficial interest which he or she receives under the deceased's will (apart from personal chattels) must be brought into account against the statutory legacy payable to the surviving spouse under the intestacy rules. Note in particular the case of *Re Bowen-Burscarlet* (1970).

The deceased's issue

Section 49(1) provides that the hotchpot rules in s 47(1)(iii) (which apply where a person dies wholly intestate having made an *inter vivos* gift to his child) apply to any benefits conferred by the will of a person who dies partially intestate to his issue.

This provision has been judicially characterised by Danckwerts J in *Re Morton* (1956) as a piece of bad draftsmanship and the problem is compounded by the fact that the courts have placed two different constructions on the provision.

On the one hand, there is the *stirpital construction* which was articulated in *Re Young* (1951) and later adopted in cases like *Re Morton* (1956) and *Re Grover's WT* (1971). The stirpital construction prescribes that any child or remoter issue of the deceased who obtains a benefit under his will must bring this into account for the purpose of determining what share that branch will take in the part of the deceased's estate not disposed of by will. In other words, *'each child [of the deceased] ought to bring into hotchpot the value of the interest actually received by such child or his or her issue'* (*per* Danckwerts J in *Re Morton*).

On the other hand, there is *the distributive construction* which was proffered by Pennycuick J in *Re Grover's WT* as an alternative to the stirpital construction. In his words, the effect of the distributive construction is that *'where any descendant of the deceased acquires a benefit under his will, he will be required to bring that interest and nothing more into account in determining his share under the partial intestacy'*.

On the weight of judicial authority, it seems that the stirpital rather than the distributive construction represents the current position of the law.

6 Provision for the deceased's family and dependants

Introduction

Although it is the prerogative of every testator to make a will in which he disposes of his property as he wishes, English law no longer permits complete testamentary freedom. Such freedom was first curtailed by Inheritance (Family Provision) Act 1938 which has now been superseded by Inheritance (Provision for Family and Dependants) Act (or I(PFD)A 1975) as amended by Law Reform Succession Act (1995).

The I(PFD)A enables close relatives and dependants of a deceased person to apply to the court for reasonable financial provision (rfp) out of the deceased's estate whether he left a will or died wholly or partially intestate. We shall refer to an applicant under the Act as A and to the deceased as D.

Applications must ordinarily be made no more than six months from the date on which a grant of administration was made (see s 4). A pr who distributes the estate within this period, may be personally liable if A's application is ultimately successful. Once the period elapses and no application has been made, the pr will no longer be liable for distributing the estate.

In exceptional circumstances, however, the court may permit an application to be made out of time. In *Re Salmon* (1980) and *Re Dennis* (1981), the courts laid down the following guidelines for determining whether to grant such permission:

- The court's jurisdiction is unfettered and is to be exercised in accordance with what is just and proper.
- The burden of proving that it is just and proper to grant an extension lies with A.
- Regard will be had to how promptly and in what circumstances the extension is sought, and in particular to such matters as the reason for the delay and whether A indicated his intention to apply under the Act before the time limit expired.
- Account will also be taken of whether any negotiations were commenced within the time limit and were still in progress when it expired.
- It will also be relevant whether or not D's estate has been distributed before A gave notice of his intention to apply under the Act. Where it has, the court will consider any hardship which may be caused to those who have benefited from distribution if A's claim is upheld.
- It will also be considered whether A will have a claim against any other party (eg his solicitor for professional negligence) if leave to apply out of time is refused.
- The court must be satisfied that A has at least an arguable case that he is entitled to rfp out of D's estate.

Recent cases which leave to apply out of time was granted include *Re (Deceased) Leave to Apply for Provision* (1995) and *Re W A (A Minor)* (1995). In both cases the decisive factors which persuaded the courts to grant the leave sought were that:

- each applicant was a minor and the delay in bringing the actions was not the fault of either but of their respective mothers who were acting on their behalf; and

- the circumstances of both applications and the size of the deceased's estate in each case were such that there was a substantial chance of success if the applications were heard.

Persons who may apply

A person is eligible to apply for rfp if he comes within any of the six categories set out in s 1(1) I(PFD)A 1975, as amended by the Law Reform (Succession) Act 1995.

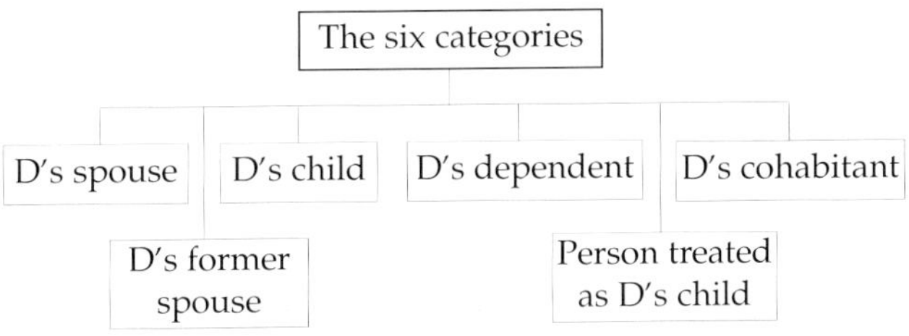

Whichever category is appropriate, A's entitlement is personal to him. Consequently, if A dies before an order for rfp is made in his favour, his pr cannot pursue the application on behalf of his estate (see *Whytte v Ticehurst* (1986); *Re R (Deceased)* (1986) and *Re Bramwell* (1988)).

Category 1: The wife or husband of the deceased (s 1(1)(a))

A will be able to claim under this heading if there was a subsisting marriage between A and D at the time D died. *Note* that:

- A subsisting marriage includes a polygamous marriage validly contracted in a foreign country (see *Re Sehota* (1978)).

- It can be deduced for s 1(2)(a) that a surviving spouse includes one who was separated from D at the time of his or her death (except where such a spouse is barred from making an application under the I(PFD)A or excluded by a court order made on the separation or thereafter).
- Under s 25(4), a party to a void marriage contracted in good faith also qualifies as a spouse of a subsisting marriage unless:
  - the marriage was dissolved/annulled in D's lifetime;
  - or the other party remarried in the D's lifetime.

Category 2: A former wife or husband of the deceased (s 1(1)(b))
An application can be made under this heading where:

- A had been validly married to D;
- the marriage was dissolved or annulled under British law or the law of a foreign country which is recognised as valid under British law;
- A did not remarry before or after D died.

(*By contrast,* remarriage does not disqualify a surviving spouse.)

A is, however, precluded from applying under this heading where he or she was barred from doing so by a court order made on the dissolution/annulment of the marriage or thereafter.

Category 3: A child of the deceased (s 1(1)(c))
In the present context, a child includes:

- a child who was *en ventre sa mère* when D died;
- an illegitimate child of D; or

- a child adopted by D (see *Williams v Johns* (1988)); but not a stepchild who has not been formally adopted.

The 1938 Act excluded applications from adult sons and married daughters unless physical or mental incapacity made them unable to maintain themselves. The 1975 Act has no such restriction but the courts have established that an adult able-bodied child of D who is capable of earning his living will be entitled to rfp only in exceptional circumstances; eg where D was paying for the child's education or where the child gave up a career to care for D during illness or old age (see *Re Coventry* (1980); *Re Rowlands* (1984); *Re Jennings* (1994) and *Goodchild v Goodchild* (1995)).

Category 4: Any person (not being the deceased's child) treated by the deceased as a child of his or her marriage (s 1(1)(d))

The usual context in which applications are made under this heading is where the relationship between D and A is that of stepparent and stepchild (see *Re Leach* (1985) (step-daughter) and *Re Callaghan* (1985) (stepson)).

It is not, however, a specific condition that A must be D's stepchild. This suggests that any other child living in D's household without being formally adopted may well apply under this heading.

Elaborating on the requirement that A must have been treated as a child of D's marriage, Slade J emphasised in *Re Leach* (1985) that mere displays of affection, kindness or hospitality by D towards A will not suffice. D must have gone further to assume the position and the attendant responsibilities and privileges of a parent towards A, either expressly or by implication.

Category 5: Other persons being maintained wholly or in part by the deceased (s 1(1)(e))

Various persons who fall outside the above categories have been held to be entitled to rfp under this heading eg: D's mistress (see *Malone v Harrison* (1979) and *Bishop v Plumley* (1991)) and D's sister (see *Re Wilkinson* (1978)).

An application can be made under s 1(1)(e) even if A and D were not residing in the same household. In *Malone v Harrison*, for example, D had set up his mistress, A, in her own house and visited her regularly while living with his wife in the matrimonial home.

Two conditions must be met before a claim will succeed under this heading:

- A must have been maintained by D wholly or in part at the time D died. In this connection A must establish that immediately before D died, (s)he was contributing substantially in money or money's worth towards A's reasonable needs.

  The effect of this requirement is seen in cases like *Kourkgy v Lusher* (1981) and *Layton v Martin* (1986). In both cases, A had been D's mistress. In each case, D had, sometime before dying, discontinued the relationship and ceased to pay for A's upkeep. This led the courts to reject the claims of both mistresses.

- It must be shown that A did not give D full valuable consideration for such maintenance. This means that a claim will not lie if the basis upon which maintenance was provided was purely contractual (eg where A was D's housekeeper and D, in return for A's services, provided her with lodgings and a salary).

This requirement has given rise to problems in instances where A and D were living together at D's death in a settled domestic relationship with each contributing substantially, financially or otherwise, towards the well-being of the other. In *Re Beaumont* (1980), where such a situation arose, it was held that A was not eligible to apply under this heading because he had provided full value for the benefits which he had derived from D in her lifetime and so was not being maintained by D.

A more flexible approach was, however, adopted in *Bishop v Plumley* (1991) where A had been D's mistress for several years during which D had provided A with a secure home and a livelihood, while A not only kept home for D but nursed him devotedly through bouts of illness, the last of which led to his death. It was held that A's contributions to D's well-being, though substantial, did not constitute full valuable consideration for the maintenance which D had provided. A's claim for rfp was therefore upheld.

Category 6: A person co-habiting with the deceased in the same household

In view of the difficulty encountered by co-habitants who had contributed substantially to their deceased partner's welfare, the Law Commission in its 1989 Report on Distribution on Intestacy, recommended that they should constitute a new category of applicants in their own right.

This proposal has been implemented by s 2 Law Reform (Succession) Act which provides that in cases where D dies after December 1995, an application for rfp may be made by any person who during the two years immediately preceding D's death was living in the same household as D as if he or she was D's wife or husband.

Applications under this heading will not fail merely because both co-habitants shared the domestic expenses (as in *Re Beaumont*) or because the surviving co-habitant contributed in kind to the other's welfare while he was still alive (as was the case in *Bishop v Plumley*).

Reasonable financial provision

Where reasonable financial provision (rfp) has, in the court's view, been made for A under D's will, intestacy or both, A's application immediately fails. See, eg *Davis v Davis* (1993) and *Rhodes v Dean* (1996). Where rfp has not been made for A, the court will then proceed to determine what amounts to rfp in the case before it.

Standards for assessing rfp (s 1(2))

The 1975 Act lays down two standards for assessing what constitutes rfp. The standard to be adopted in any given case depends on the heading under which A brings his application.

The two standards

- The 'surviving spouse' standard: Where A comes within category 1
- The 'maintenance' standard: Where A applies under any other category

In applying these two standards, the courts adopt an objective approach. This means in effect that:

- they do not rely exclusively on the facts and circumstances known to D but also take due account of other material facts and circumstances (see *Re Goodwin* (1969) and *Re Shanahan* (1973));

- they do not base their judgment on the facts as they stood at D's death but on the facts prevailing at the date of the hearing (see s 3(5)).

The surviving spouse standard

Where A is a surviving spouse, rfp means such financial provision as it would be reasonable in all the circumstances of the case for a husband or wife to receive *whether or not that provision is required for [A's] maintenance.*

The surviving spouse standard is more favourable than the maintenance standard. The object of introducing the surviving spouse standard was to enable the court to assess the entitlement of the surviving spouse under the Act on the same footing as it would have done if the marriage had been terminated by divorce rather than death (see *Re Bunning* (1984); *Re Besterman* (1984); *Kusminow v Barclays Bank* (1989) and *Moody v Stephenson* (1992)).

The position of a judicially separated/former spouse: An application by a judicially separated or former spouse is normally dealt with on the basis of the maintenance standard. The court, however, has the discretion to adopt the surviving spouse standard when dealing with such an application provided:

- D died within 12 months of the grant of the decree of divorce or judicial separation; and
- no application was made for financial provision during the relevant proceedings or an application was made but had not been determined at D's death (see s 14).

The maintenance standard

This applies in all other cases. Under this standard, rfp means 'such financial provision as it would be reasonable in all the circumstances of the case for A to receive *for his maintenance*.

In this context, maintenance connotes 'payments which, directly or indirectly, enable A to discharge the cost of his daily living at whatever standard is appropriate to him. The provision to be made is to meet recurring expenses being expenses of living of an income nature' (*per* Browne-Wilkinson J in *Re Dennis*).

The appropriate level of maintenance depends on the facts and circumstances of each case. As Goff J observed in *Re Coventry* (1980), 'it does not mean just enough to enable [A] to get by; on the other hand, it does not mean anything which may be regarded as reasonably desirable for his general welfare or benefit' (see to the same effect *Re Leach*).

The guidelines for assessing what constitutes rfp

The material factors which a court must take into account in deciding what provision should be made for A, are to be found in the guidelines laid down in s 3.

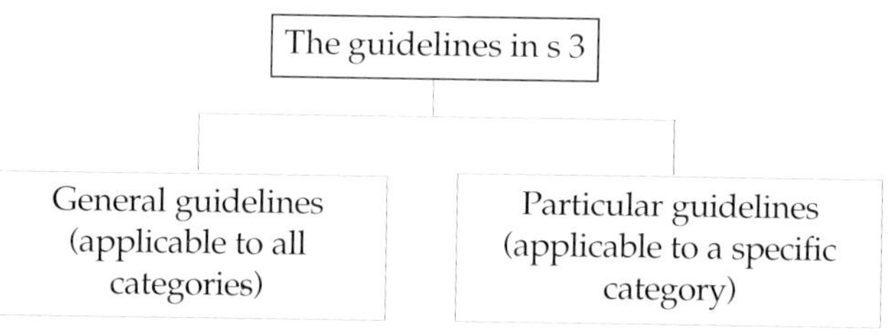

The General Guidelines

Material factors	Comment
1 Existing and future financial resources and needs of: – the applicant; – any other applicant; – any beneficiaries under D's will or intestacy.	• In assessing these resources, account is taken of current earnings/earning capacity; money in the bank; capital assets and assets likely to mature in the future; eg endowment policies. • In assessing these needs, account is taken of all responsibilities and obligations of the party concerned; eg school fees, mortgage repayments; number of dependants etc.
2 Responsibilities and obligations owed by D to any applicant or beneficiary under his will or intestacy.	Such obligations have been held to be owed to: • wife of many years: *Re Besterman;* • sick daughter: *Re Debenham* (1986); • elderly mother: *Re Clarke* (1968); • mistress of 20 years: *Re Joslin* (1941). No obligation found towards; • adult able-bodied son: *Re Coventry;*

	• daughter who left home many years ago: *Re Andrews* (1951); • wife who deserted husband: *Re Gregory* (1971); • adopted daughter whose lifestyle had alienated her from D: *Re Collins*.
3 Size and nature of D's estate.	• If D's estate is sizeable, the provision for A is likely to be more than if small: compare award of £378,000 to spouse in *Besterman* with £45,000 award in *Kusminow*. • However, the fact that the estate is small does not in itself exclude A from claiming rfp: *Re Clayton* (1966).
4 Physical or mental inability of an applicant or beneficiary.	• It was held in *Re Wood* (1980) and *Re Debenham* that presence of severe disability enables adult child of deceased to claim rfp. • It was held in *Re Watkins* (1949), where A's incapacity entitled him to state aid, that no provision should be made for A out of D's estate.

	By contrast, *Re Pringle* (1946) and *Millward v Shenton* (1972) held that A was entitled to rfp out of D's estate although A was in receipt of state aid for his disability.
5 Other matters which the court considers relevant including the conduct of A or any other person.	• As regards conduct, the cases indicate that where A was particularly devoted to D when he was alive, this will count in A's favour: *Re Cooke* (1955); *Re Callaghan*; *Malone v Harrison* and *Bishop v Plumley*. Contrast, however, with *Re Collins* where A's bad conduct was considered equally relevant. • One other material factor in the present context is the source of D's wealth. For example, if D's wife died before D leaving her estate to D and he dies without providing in his will for A who is a child of the marriage, the fact that D's estate was derived in part from A's mother will be relevant in assessing A's entitlement: *Sivyer v Sivyer* (1967) and *Goodchild v Goodchild*.

The Particular Guidelines

Category of applicant	Material factors
1 Surviving spouse.	• A's age and duration of the marriage. • The contribution made by A to the welfare of D's family including looking after the home. • The amount A might reasonably have expected to receive if the marriage had been dissolved when D died (the *imaginary divorce guideline*). The operation of this guideline is illustrated by cases like *Re Bunning; Re Besterman; Kusminow v Barclays Bank* and *Moody v Stephenson*.
2 Judicially separated or former spouse.	• A's age and duration of the marriage. • A's contribution to the welfare of D's family. *Note* also that the court will consider any financial settlement between A and D at the time of the dissolution/judicial separation or thereafter: *Re Fullard* (1981) and *Cameron v Treasury Solicitor* (1996).

3 D's child.	• The manner in which A was being or might expect to be educated or trained.
4 Person treated by D as child of the family.	• Whether D assumed responsibility for maintaining A, and if so, the basis, extent and duration of such maintenance. • Whether in assuming such responsibility, D knew that A was not actually his child. • Whether any other person is responsible for A's maintenance.
5 Any other dependant maintained by D.	• The extent to which D assumed responsibility for A's maintenance. • The basis upon which D assumed responsibility. • The length of time for which D discharged this responsibility.
6 Co-habitants.	• A's age and the length of time for which A lived with D as husband and wife in the same household. • A's contributions to the welfare of D's family, including looking after the home or caring for the family.

Orders which the court may make (s 2(1))

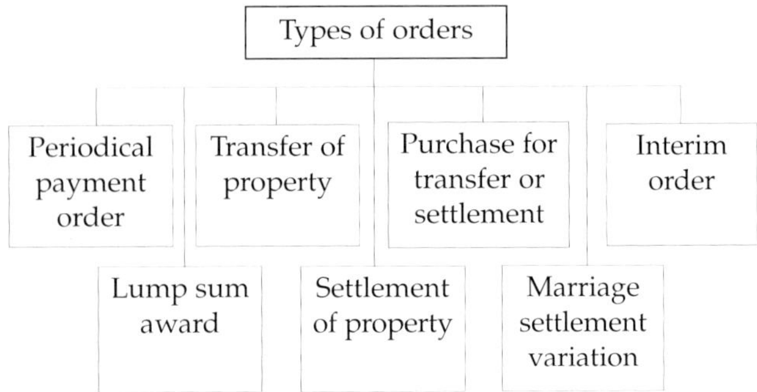

Periodical payments

An order of this nature may entail:

- payments of specified amounts at periodic intervals (eg £100 per month to be paid to A);
- payments equal to the whole or a specified part of the income of the net estate of the deceased (eg the income from one-third of the net estate to be paid to A);
- payments equal to the whole income of such part of the net estate as the court directs to be set aside or appropriated (eg the court may order £10,000 to be set aside and invested and the income produced to be paid to A).
- in the alternative, the court may direct the periodical payments to be determined in any other manner it sees fit.

The order will normally state the duration for which the payments are to run. This may be a fixed number of years; for the rest of A's life; or until A attains majority, marries or re-marries, as appropriate. In the case of judicially separated/former spouses, s 19(2) provides that an order for periodical payments automatically terminates on re-marriage.

Variation and discharge of periodical payment orders
Applications to vary, discharge, suspend or revive a suspended periodical payment order may be made by any of the following parties:

- A, for whose benefit the order was made or any other person who has applied or would be entitled to apply for an order but for the time limit in s 4;
- D's personal representatives;
- the trustee of any property which is subject to the periodical payment order; or
- any beneficiary under the deceased's will or intestacy.

Lump sum payments
The court may order a once and for all lump sum to be paid to A out of D's net estate. Once a lump sum payment has been ordered, A cannot return to court for any other relief. Hence, it was signified in *Re Besterman* that in fixing the lump sum, the court must take due account of the effects of inflation and other contingencies that might affect A's circumstances.

The court may order the lump sum to be paid to A in instalments. Where this is the case, the court may subsequently vary the number of instalments payable and the dates on which they are to be paid, but not the amount of the lump sum.

Transfer of property

The personal representatives may be ordered to transfer any property forming part of the deceased's net estate to A. This is usually favoured in cases where ordering a lump sum payment would entail an unnecessary sale of assets comprised in the estate.

Settlement of property

The court is also empowered to order the settlement of any property forming part of the deceased's net estate for the benefit of A. In this event, the property will not be transferred to A himself, but to trustees on his behalf. This order is especially appropriate where, by reason of infancy or some other reason, A is incapable of managing his own affairs.

Acquisition of property for transfer or settlement

The court may order specified property to be paid for out of the deceased's net estate and either transferred to or settled on trust for A.

Variation of marriage settlement

The court may make an order varying any ante-nuptial or post-nuptial settlement made in connection with the marriage of D. The variation can only be ordered if A, for whose benefit it is made, is the surviving spouse of that marriage, a child of the marriage, or any person who was treated as a child of the family in relation to the marriage.

The effect of an order

Where an order is made under the Act, the effect of this is that for all purposes, D's will or the law governing the devolution of D's property on intestacy are deemed to operate subject to the terms of the order. Consequently, A, in whose favour the order was made, is treated as the equivalent of a beneficiary under a will or intestacy.

In making the order, the court may require any person holding any property which forms part of the deceased's estate to make such payment or transfer such property as is necessary to fulfil the terms of the order, whether that person holds the property as a personal representative or in any other capacity.

The court may make an order expressly varying the terms of D's will or the operation of the intestacy rules in whatever manner it thinks is fair and just. For example, if the court makes an order transferring a house forming part of D's estate to A and the property in question was specifically left to a named devisee in D's will, the court may at the same time vary the terms of the will with a view to making some other provision for that devisee.

Interim orders

Under s 5 of the Act, the court may make an interim order in A's favour. The need for such orders stems from the fact that a full hearing of the application may take a fairly long time and in the meantime A, having been dependent on D when D was alive, may be in financial difficulty.

Two conditions must be established before an interim order will be granted:

- A must be in immediate need of financial assistance;
- there must be property forming part of D's net estate which is available to meet this need.

When a final order is eventually made after a full hearing, it is open to the court to direct that whatever A received under the interim order be brought into account against the amount awarded to A under the final order.

The deceased's 'net estate'

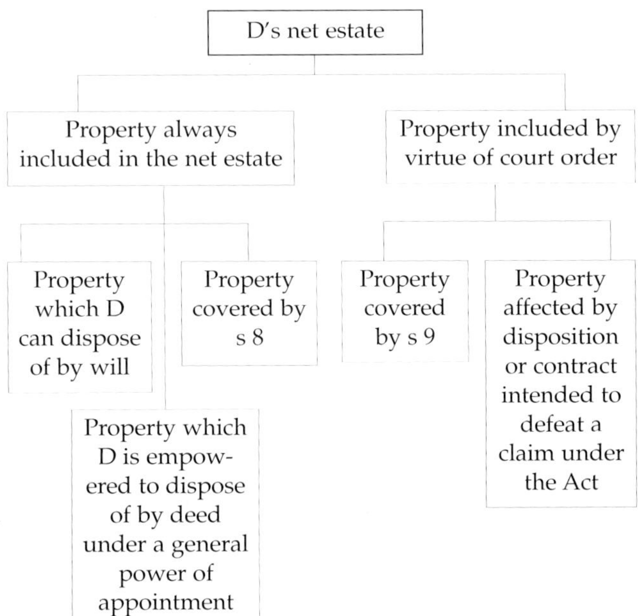

When a court makes any order for financial provision under the Act, this must come out of D's net estate. Section 25 of the Act identifies various categories of property which fall within the net estate, namely:

Property always included in the net estate

- All property which D has power to *dispose of by his will* (other than by virtue of a *special power of appointment*), less whatever amount may be needed for:

(i) funeral, testamentary and administration expenses;

(ii) the payment of the deceased's debts and liabilities; and

(iii) the payment of inheritance tax.

- Any property in respect of which D held a *general power of appointment* exercisable by deed which was not exercised in his lifetime. If the power was exercisable by will, it falls within the first category.
- Any sum of money or other property covered by s 8, namely:
  - money or property which is the subject of a *statutory nomination* made by D in favour of any person; or
  - D's money or property which was given to any person under a *donatio mortis causa*.

Property included in the net estate if the court so orders

- The court may, by virtue of s 9, order D's severable share of any property of which he was a beneficial joint tenant at his death to be treated as part of his net estate. For example, if D and another person, X, were beneficial joint tenants of a house or a chose in action (eg money in a joint bank account) immediately before D's death, X becomes entitled to the property under the right of survivorship. The court may, however, order that D's severable share of the property shall be treated as part of his net estate to such extent as appears just in the circumstances (see, eg *Jessop v Jessop* (1992) and *Powell v Osbourne* (1993)).
- Under s 10, the court may set aside a disposition of property made by D less than six years before his death in favour of a person who did not give full valuable

consideration, if it appears that the disposition was intended to defeat possible applications for financial provision under the Act.

Again, under s 11, the court may set aside a contract made by D in which he agreed to leave a sum of money or other property (or agreed that a sum of money or other property would be paid or transferred out of his estate) to a person who did not give full valuable consideration, if the court concludes that the contract was made to defeat possible applications under the Act.

Where a disposition or contract is set aside on these grounds, the court may order that the property or sum of money to which it relates is to form part of D's estate for the purpose of satisfying any provision to which A is entitled under the Act.

7 Administration of the deceased's estate

The process of becoming a personal representative

The responsibility of administering a deceased person's estate rests with his personal representative (pr).

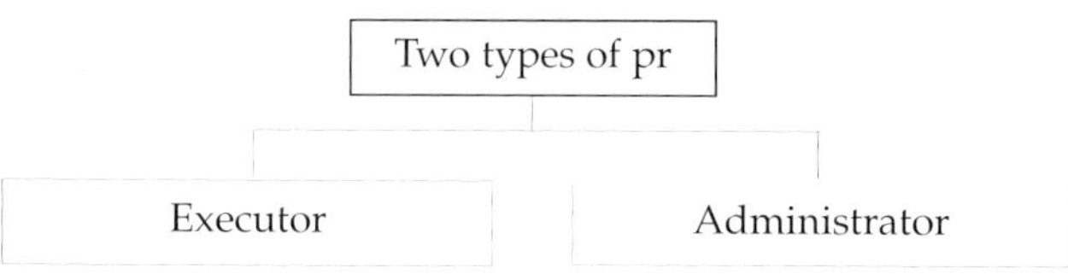

Executors

Executors are persons appointed to carry out the terms of a will.

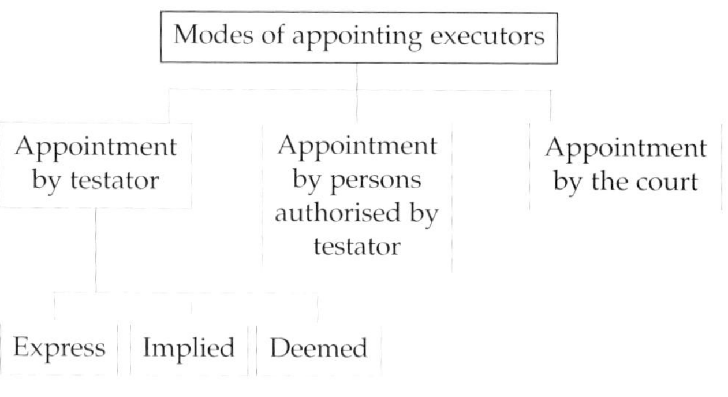

Appointment by testator

Express appointment: It is T's prerogative to appoint executors in his will. The appointment may be *absolute* or it may be *qualified* by imposing various conditions or restrictions, eg that the executor:

- must fulfil certain criteria before assuming office;
- will cease to hold office on the happening of specified events;
- is a *special* executor appointed to administer certain assets;
- is a substitute who will be eligible to act only if some other executor is unable or unwilling to do so (see *In the Goods of Betts* (1861) and *In the Goods of Foster* (1871)).

Implied appointment: This occurs where a person not expressly named as an executor is instructed in the will to act with the executor (as was the case in *In the Goods of Brown* (1902)); or is entrusted with duties ordinarily performed by a testator (as was the case in *In the Goods of Adamson* (1875) and *In the Goods of Cook* (1902)). Such a person is known as executor according to the tenor of the will.

Deemed appointment: Under s 22 AEA, where settled land which was vested in T at his death remains settled land after T dies, the trustees of the settlement are deemed to have been appointed in T's will as special executives with regard to such settled land.

Appointment by persons authorised by testator

T may in his will authorise other persons to appoint executors on his behalf. Such an appointment is as effective as one made by T himself (see *In the Goods of Ryder* (1861); *In the Goods of Cringan* (1828) and *In the Goods of Deichmann* (1842)).

Appointment by the court

A court may appoint executors under the powers conferred on it by statute, eg s 50 AJA 1985 (appointment of substitute executors); and s 114 SCA 1981 (appointment of additional executors where there is only one).

Transmission of office

Where an executor has begun administering T's estate but dies before completing the task, s 7 AEA provides for the *automatic transmission* of his office to an *executor by representation*. For example:

If T died in 1993 having appointed E1 as his sole executor and soon after obtaining probate E1 died in 1994 having appointed E2 as his executor, once E2 obtains probate of E1's will, he becomes T's executor by representation.

There can be no transmission of office once the chain of representation is broken. In our example, this would happen if E1:

- died intestate;
- made a will without naming an executor; or
- named E2 as his executor but E2 made a disclaimer or died without obtaining probate of E1's will.

The number of executors

There is no *lower limit* on the number of executors. There is also no upper limit on the number of executors appointed in a will. However, if more than four are appointed, s 114(1) SCA 1981 provides that probate shall be granted to four of them with a *power reserved* to the others to apply for probate if any of these four ceases to hold office.

Capacity

- A *minor* cannot obtain probate until his majority (rr 32 and 33 NC Prob Rules 1987 and s 118 SCA 1981). Again, a person who is *physically* or *mentally incapable* cannot act as an executor (see *Evans v Tyler* (1849); and *In the Goods of Galbraith* (1951)).
- A *corporation sole* (eg the Public Trustee) may be an executor and obtain probate in the corporate name (see *In the Goods of Haynes* (1842)). A *trust corporation* (eg the Executor and Trustee Department of a bank) is also empowered by s 115(1) SCA 1981 to act as an executor and obtain probate in its own name. Initially, the corporation had to be constituted under UK law (see *Re Barlow* (1933)); but this no longer appears to be the case (see *Re Bigger* (1977)).
- Where a will appoints a *firm* as executors with nothing more, the issue arises as to whether T meant the partners at the date of the will or of his death (see *In the Goods of Fernie* (1849)). This problem may be averted by an appropriate clause; eg 'I appoint the partners of X firm at the date of my death to be the executors of my will'.

Passing over

Under s 116 SCA 1981, a court may in special circumstances pass over an executor and appoint any person it thinks suitable as an administrator in his place. See, for example:

Case	Reason for passing over
In the Goods of Wright (1898)	Executor could not be found.
In the Estate of Potticary (1927)	Executor's bad character.
In Re S (1968)	Executrix in prison for life.
In the Estate of Biggs (1966)	Executor's persistent refusal to obtain probate.

Renunciation of probate

A person appointed as an executor may *renounce* probate (see *Doyle v Blake* (1804)). This must be done in writing and must be filed in a probate registry.

A renunciation may be retracted before filing (see *In the Goods of Morant* (1874)). After filing, it can only be retracted with the Registrar's leave under r 37(3) NC Prob Rules 1987 (see *In the Goods of Stiles* (1898) and *In the Goods of Gill* (1873)).

Acceptance

An executor is deemed to accept office where he:

- obtains a grant of probate; or
- *intermeddles* in the testator's estate without obtaining a grant. Acts which have been held to constitute intermeddling include:

Case	Nature of act
Pytt v Fendall (1754)	Release of debt due to estate.
Long v Symes (1832)	Advertising for claims against estate.
Re Stevens (1897)	Request for payment of insurance money due to the estate.

Other acts which have been held not to amount to intermeddling include:

Case	Nature of act
Harrison v Rowley (1798)	Arranging testator's funeral.
Rayner v Green (1839)	Dealing with estate as agent.
Holder v Holder (1968)	Signing cheques for small amounts and endorsing a few insurance policies.

Note, once acceptance is effective the executor can no longer renounce probate (see *In the Goods of Veiga* (1862)).

Citations: Where a person appointed as an executor makes no effort to assume office, the person who would be entitled to administer the estate if that executor renounced probate may apply under r 47(1) NC Prob Rules for a citation requiring the executor to renounce or accept probate.

Where an executor who has intermeddled with the estate omits or refuses to obtain probate, a citation may be made under r 47(1) requiring him to appear in court and show good cause why he should not be compelled to obtain probate.

Administrators

An administrator will be appointed to administer the estate of a deceased person who left no will or left a will but no executors.

Grant with will annexed

Where there is a will but no executors, there will be a grant of administration with the will annexed. The persons entitled to the grant will be determined by the order of priority set out in r 20 NC Prob Rules 1978, namely:

- trustees of the residuary estate for the benefit of others;
- residuary legatees and devisees, including those entitled to a life interest in the residuary estate (and in cases where the residue is not wholly disposed of under the will, those entitled to share in the undisposed of residue under the intestacy rules);
- the pr of a residuary legatee or devisee or person entitled to a share in any residue not disposed of by will (except where such a legatee or devisee is entitled to a life interest

in the residuary estate or is a trustee for some other person);

- other legatees or devisees, including those entitled to a life interest or who are holding on trust for any such other legatees or devisees, as well as the creditors of the deceased;
- the prs of such legatees/devisees who have died (except where the devisee or legatee is entitled to a life interest) as well as the prs of creditors who have died.

Simple grant

Where the deceased died without leaving a valid will, there will be a simple grant. Under r 22 NC Prob Rules, applicants for such a grant are placed in the following order of priority:

- the surviving spouse of the deceased;
- the children of the deceased and, in the case of a child of the deceased who died before the deceased, the issue of such child;
- the parents of the deceased;
- the deceased's brothers and sisters of the whole blood and the issue of any such brother or sister who died before the deceased;
- the deceased's brothers and sisters of the half blood and the issue of any such brother or sister who died before the deceased;
- the grandparents of the deceased;
- the deceased's uncles and aunts of the whole blood and the issue of any such uncle or aunt who died before the deceased;

- the deceased's uncles and aunts of the half blood and the issue of any such uncle or aunt who died before the deceased.

A person within any of these categories can obtain a grant only if he actually has a beneficial interest in the estate. Thus, if D dies intestate survived by children, his parents are not entitled to a grant as the entire estate devolves on D's children.

Where the deceased is survived by nobody within these categories, his estate passes to the Crown as *bona vacantia* and a grant will be made to the Treasury Solicitor on the Crown's behalf (see, eg *Cameron v Treasury Solicitor* (1996)).

Clearing off

Whether r 20 or r 22 applies, a person with a prior right to administration may be *cleared off* where he is dead, has renounced his right or has been issued a citation requiring him to accept or renounce the grant and has declined to accept. Where all those with prior rights are cleared off, this enables a person who is lower down in the order to apply for a grant.

Entitlement in the same degree

Where there are several persons entitled in the same degree, either under r 20 or r 22, any of them may obtain a grant without being required to give notice to the others.

To safeguard against this possibility, it is open to any person entitled to a grant to enter a caveat. Once he does so, he has to be notified before any grant is made.

The number of administrators

Under s 114(1) SCA, administration will not be granted to more than *four persons* in respect of the same part of the deceased's estate. Where there are *minor* beneficiaries or a life interest involved, s 114(2) provides that the grant must be made to at least two individuals (or a *trust corporation*) unless the court directs otherwise.

Capacity

The capacity to be an administrator is determined by rules similar to those applicable to executors (which have been outlined at p 118 above).

Passing over

By virtue of s 116 SCA, a person who would otherwise be entitled to a grant of administration may be passed over in the same manner as an executor; see, for example:

Case	Reason for passing over
In the Goods of Ardern (1898)	Person entitled was a drunkard.
In the Goods of Caldicott (1899)	Person entitled had gone missing.
In the Goods of Clowhill (1866)	Person entitled was in foreign land.

But *note, In the Goods of Edward-Taylor* (1951) where the court declined to pass over a young lady entitled to a grant as sole beneficiary on the ground that she was immature for her age and likely to dissipate her inheritance.

Acceptance

Acceptance occurs where a person entitled to a grant of administration obtains a grant. Unlike the position in the case of an executor, the fact that a person carries out the functions of an administrator will not amount to acceptance on his part (see *In the Goods of Davis* (1860) and *In the Goods of Fell* (1861)).

Renunciation

A person who is entitled to a grant may renounce his entitlement before such a grant is made. This must be done in writing and filed with the Probate Registrar. Once a renunciation is filed, it can only be *retracted* with the leave of the court.

Citations

Where a person entitled to administration takes no steps either to accept or to renounce office, the court may issue a citation to compel him to do one or the other.

Revocation of grants

A pr remains in office until the administration of the estate is completed unless the grant of probate or administration is revoked.

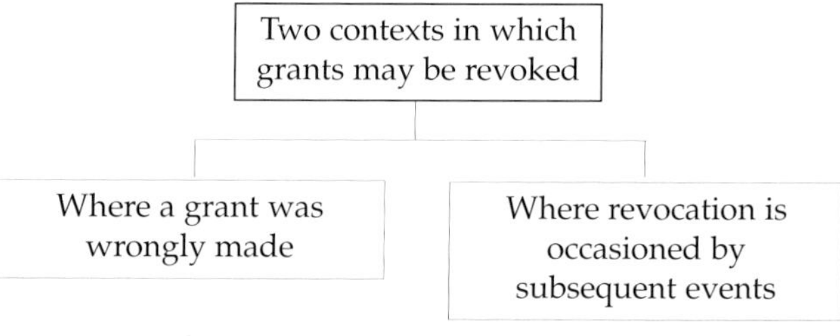

Where a grant was wrongly made

Section 121(1) SCA 1981 empowers the court to revoke a grant 'where it appears that ... it ought not to have been made or contains an error'. See, for example:

Case	Reason for revocation
In the Goods of Napier (1839) *In the Goods of Bloch* (1959)	Person whose estate was to be administered was still alive.
In the Goods of Bergman (1842) *In the Goods of Moore* (1845)	Person to whom grant was made not eligible.
Priestman v Thomas (1884)	Grant made under a will that was later found to be invalid.

Revocation occasioned by subsequent events

A grant which was properly made may be revoked in response to various events. See, for example:

Case	Nature of revoking event
In the Goods of Galbraith	Pr too old to continue in office.
In the Goods of Thacker (1900)	Pr who took out grant as trustee in bankruptcy discharged after all debts were paid.
In the Estate of Thomas (1912)	Emigration of pr to New Zealand.
In the Goods of Loveday (1900)	Serious breach of duty by pr.

The effect of revocation

- Under s 37(1) AEA, conveyances of real or personal property made by a pr whose grant is later revoked remain valid in spite of the revocation. Although the provision does not apply to transfers other than by conveyance, the effect of the decision in *Hewson v Shelley* (1914) appears to be that such a transfer also remains valid, where it was to a purchaser for value who took it in good faith.

- Under s 39(1)(iii) AEA, a contract made by a pr before his grant is revoked remains enforceable by/against his successor(s) in office.
- Under s 27(2) AEA, all payments and dispositions made to the pr in good faith before revocation are a valid discharge to the person making them if the grant is revoked.
- Under s 27(1) AEA, if the pr paid money or distributed property out of the deceased's estate in good faith before the revocation, he will not be liable in respect of the payment or distribution (see *In the Estate of Bloch*).

Different effects of probate and letters of administration

Although executors and administrators are both charged with the responsibility of administering the estates of deceased persons, several significant differences arise from the fact that the executor derives his authority from the will as seen from cases like *Chetty v Chetty* (1916) and *Biles v Ceasar* (1957); while the administrator derives his authority from the grant.

The time at which property vests

The estate ordinarily vests in the executor when T dies (see *Woolley v Clark* (1882) and *Chetty v Chetty*)). By contrast, under s 9 AEA, the deceased's property only vests in the administrator after the grant is made. Before then, it vests in the public trustee.

The doctrine of *relation back* was, however, evolved by the courts as a device for safeguarding the estate of the deceased in the interval between his death and the date on which the administrator obtained his grant. By virtue of this doctrine, once the grant was made to the administrator, this entitled him to take legal action in respect of unlawful acts committed after the deceased died but before the grant (see *Foster v Bates* (1843) and *Re Pryse* (1904)).

Litigation before grant

An executor may commence legal proceedings in respect of T's estate even before obtaining probate (see *Easton v Carter* (1850); *Chetty v Chetty* and *Re Crowhurst Park* (1974)). An administrator cannot, however, institute proceedings until he obtains a grant (see *Ingall v Moran* (1944)).

Acts of administration before the grant is made

Even before obtaining probate, an executor can do all things executors are entitled to do in respect of T's estate except those that require a grant of probate in order to prove title (see, eg *Re Stevens* (1897) and *Wankford v Wankford* (1704). He may for instance:

- take possession of assets belonging to T;
- receive or release debts owed to T's estate and pay his debts;
- sell and transfer assets belonging to T's estate to purchasers;
- pay legacies or transfer property given under T's will to the intended beneficiaries.

By contrast, an administrator has no right to perform any of these functions until the grant has been made (see *Wankford v Wankford*; *Holland v King* (1848) and *Mills v Anderson* (1984)).

Executorship by representation

There is one notable difference between the position of executors and administrators in the period after a grant. This stems from the fact that executorship by representation, as provided for in s 7 AEA, has no place in the context of grants of administration.

In all other respects, once a grant has been made the position of an administrator is more or less the same as that of an executor, as seen from s 21 AEA.

The process of administering the estate after grant

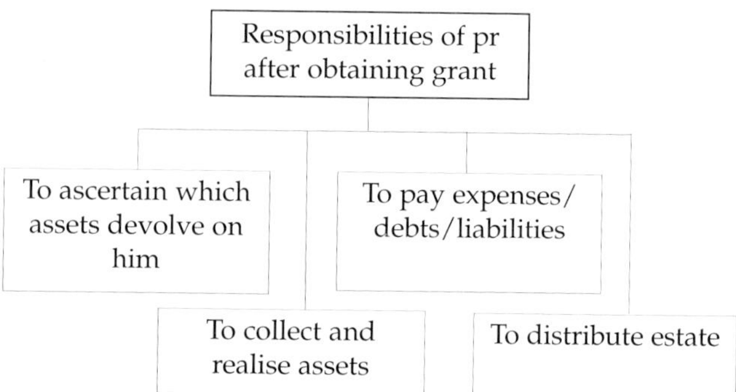

Devolution on personal representatives

Before 1926, a deceased's personal estate devolved on his prs but his real property went directly to the devisee under his will or his heir at law if he died intestate. Since the AEA 1925 was enacted, the deceased's real property now vests in his prs.

The *real estate* which vests in the prs includes:

- land held by the deceased as sole trustee on trust for sale;
- land held by the deceased as a tenant for life under a settlement (which devolves on trustees of the settlement as special prs);
- land held by the deceased by way of mortgage or security:
- land appointed by the deceased in the exercise of a general power of appointment.

Property which does not devolve on prs includes the following:

- an interest owned by the deceased which ceases on his death;
- a statutory tenancy held by the deceased under the Rents Acts;
- property transferred by the deceased under a *donatio mortis causa* which is perfected at his death (see, eg *Re Beaumont* (1902));
- insurance policies in favour of the deceased's spouse/children;
- property which has been nominated (see *Bennet v Slater* (1899); *Eccles Provident Industrial Co-op Society v Griffiths* (1912)).

Causes of action

Causes of action vested in or against a deceased at his death survive for the benefit of or against his estate under s 1(1) Law (Miscellaneous Provisions) Act (1934) (see *Otter v Church* (1953); *Cooper v Jarman* (1866); *Wantworth v Cock* (1839) and *Beswick v Beswick* (1968)).

The cause of action will not however survive the deceased where the obligation imposed on him is purely personal in nature (see *Farrow v Wilson* (1869)).

Collection and preservation of the estate

Duty to collect

Under s 25 AEA, a pr has a duty to collect the deceased's estate. He must recover assets lent or hired out by the deceased and arrears of rent due to the deceased. In particular, he must act promptly to recover unsecured debts due to the estate (see *Powell v Evans* (1802); *Caney v Bond* (1843); *Hayward v Kinsey* (1701); *Tebbs v Carpenter* (1816) and *Stiles v Guy* (1848)).

Under s 15 TA, prs may compromise or otherwise settle debts or other claims relating to the deceased's estate and are not liable for any loss to the estate provided they acted in good faith. They will, however, be liable, if the loss is due to their neglect rather than a considered exercise of the power under s 15 (see *Re Greenwood* (1911)).

Duty to preserve

The pr must also take reasonable care to preserve the deceased's assets which have come into his hands. Once he has done so, he will not be liable if the assets get lost or destroyed (see *Jones v Lewis* (1676); *Executors of the Lady Croft v Lyndsey* (1676) and *Job v Job* (1877)).

The pr is not under a strict duty to insure any of the deceased's assets unless there is a direction to this effect in his will (see *Bailey v Gould* (1840) and *Fry v Fry* (1859)). He is, however, empowered by s 19 TA to insure the deceased's buildings and other insurable assets against loss or damage by fire.

Realisation of the estate

The prs are often required to hold the deceased's estate on trust for sale by his will or under s 33 AEA, if he died intestate. By virtue of the Trusts of Land and Appointment of Trustees Act (1996), such trusts for sale have now been redesignated as trusts of land with a power of sale.

Moreover, at common law and in equity, the pr had the power to sell the deceased's personalty for the purpose of carrying out the administration of his estate (see *Nugent v Gifford* (1738); *Whale v Booth* (1789) and *Ewer v Corbett* (1723)).

A pr could also mortgage or lease the deceased's personalty for purposes of administration (see *Earl Vane v Rigden* (1870); *Scott v Tyler* (1788); *M'Leod v Drummond* (1810); *Russel v Plaice* (1854) and *Oceanic Steam Navigation Co v Sutherberry* (1880)).

More recently, s 39 AEA has given prs a power to sell, lease or mortgage the deceased's real and personal estate not only for the purpose of administration but also during the minority of any beneficiary or the subsistence of a life interest.

Carrying on the deceased's business

As a rule, prs have no authority to run the deceased's business after he dies (see *Barker v Parker* (1786) and *Kirkman v Booth* (1848)).

Note, however, that:

- the prs may carry on the business in order to meet outstanding contractual obligations (see *Marshall v Broadhurst* (1831) and *Edwards v Grace* (1836));
- the prs may carry on the business with a view to selling it as a going concern (see *Dowse v Gorton* (1891));
- the prs can carry on the business, if the deceased's will expressly allows this. It was held in *Re Crowther* (1895) that if a will contains a power to postpone the sale of the business, this implies that the prs may carry on the business pending its sale.

It was not certain whether the statutory power to postpone sale conferred on administrators by s 33 AEA also implied, by analogy to the discussion in *Re Crowther*, that they could also carry on any business forming part of an intestatee's estate. In any event, the original s 33 has now been amended pursuant to the Trusts of Land and Appointment of Trustees

Act (1996) and in its amended form it makes no reference to this power to postpone sale.

The deceased's leaseholds: Where the estate includes a leasehold interest, this devolves on the pr without any need for him to enter into possession. As soon as this happens, he becomes liable in a *representative capacity* for breaches of covenants until he assigns the lease to a beneficiary or purchaser.

When the pr enters into possession of the demised premises, he also becomes *personally liable* for rents and breaches of covenant committed while he remains in possession (see *Mayor [etc] of Stratford-upon-Avon v Parker* (1914) and *Whitehead v Palmer* (1908)).

The pr may, however, protect himself against personal liability:

- by obtaining an indemnity from the beneficiary who will become entitled to the lease when distribution occurs; or
- by setting aside an indemnity fund out of the estate.

Payment of expenses, debts and liabilities

Ascertainment of creditors

The prs must pay the expenses, debts and liabilities of the deceased with due diligence (see *Re Tankard* (1942)). Even if a will does not direct the pr to pay these debts, this duty is provided for in the AEA.

The pr has the task of ascertaining the deceased's creditors. If a debt is unpaid because the pr fails in this responsibility, he may be personally liable to the creditor (see *Knatchbull v Fearnhead* (1837)).

The pr is, however, protected against unpaid creditors once he has advertised for claims by creditors and distributed the estate in the manner prescribed by s 27 TA.

Where an advertisement of the type contemplated by s 27 is not feasible, the court may nevertheless grant the pr leave to distribute on the basis that all outstanding debts have been met (see *Re Gess* (1942)).

Funeral expenses

The prs estate must bear the cost of the funeral and a pr who pays for the funeral may recover his reasonable expenses from the estate (see *Corner v Shaw* (1838); *Goldstein v Salvation Army Assurance Society* (1917); *Gammell v Wilson* (1982) and *Re Grandison* (1989)).

Testamentary/administration expenses

These are expenses which are connected to the proper performance of a pr's duties (see *Sharp v Lush* (1879) and *Re Taylor's Estate* (1969)). Such expenses include:

Case	Nature of expense
Re Clemmow (1904)	Sum required to obtain grant.
Sharp v Lush (1879)	Sum spent on legal advice.
Miles v Harrison (1874) *Re Hall-Dare* (1916)	Cost of applying for court's directions on matters relating to the estate.
Re Goetze (1953) *Re Sebba* (1959)	Expenses incurred in collection or preservation of the estate.

Order of payment of debts where estate is solvent

If the deceased's estate is solvent, his expenses, debts and liabilities are payable in full. In determining which of his assets will be applied in the payment of these debts, etc his prs are required by s 34(3) AEA to adopt the order of abatement set out in Schedule I, Part II AEA.

Under Schedule I, Part II, debts are payable out of:

- property of the deceased *undisposed of by his will* subject to retention of a fund sufficient to meet any pecuniary legacies. *Note*, this includes not only property which T has not attempted to dispose of by will, but also property passing under a gift in the will which lapses (see *Re Lamb* (1929));
- property not specifically devised or bequeathed, but *included* either by a specific or general description in a *residuary gift*, subject to the retention out of such property of a fund sufficient to meet any pecuniary legacies so far as not provided for in the first category;
- property *specifically appropriated*, *devised* or *bequeathed* either by general or specific description for payment of debts;
- property *charged with* or *devised* or *bequeathed subject to a charge* for the payment of debts;
- the fund, if any, *retained to meet pecuniary legacies*;
- property specifically devised or bequeathed *under the will*;
- property appointed by will under a *general power of appointment*.

Note in this connection that:

- Where any asset is applied towards the payment of the deceased's debts in accordance with the above order, the interest of the person who would have been entitled to that asset abates.

- Where the assets in a given category include both real and personal property, they will abate *rateably*. This means that the burden of the deceased's debts will be borne proportionately by such real and personal property according to their value.

- Assets in a particular category must abate completely before recourse will be had to assets in the next category for the purpose of paying the deceased's debts.

- This order of payment will be varied where the deceased's will contains provisions to the contrary. Apart from instances where the will expressly provides for such variations, the courts have also recognised that an intention to vary the order may be implied from the provisions of the will. In particular:

  - In cases like *Re Harland-Peck* (1940) and *Re Petty* (1929), such an intention was implied where the will left T's residuary estate to certain beneficiaries subject to payment of T's funeral and testamentary expenses, debts, etc. The effect of this was that T's debts had to be met out of the entire residue instead of being payable primarily out of the part of the residue undisposed of by the will, as contemplated by the statutory order.

    By contrast, in *Re Lamb,* where the will directed that T's debts, etc were to be paid without indicating the property out of which payment was to be made, there was no implied variation. The property undisposed of in the will was thus primarily liable under the first category for the payment of T's debts.

- In *Re Meldrum* (1952), where T in his will gave B £500 for her immediate expenses as well as whatever was left in T's bank deposit account after all legacies, debts, etc had been met. T then left his residuary estate to B and C. The court was able to deduce from this that T intended to vary the statutory order. As a result, the money in the deposit account (which would have come after T's residuary estate if the statutory order was adopted), was primarily liable for the payment of T's debts.

However, *contrast* with *Re Gordon* (1940), where T left her executors £50 to be applied in paying her debts with the remainder to be paid to B. It was held that there was no implied intention to vary the statutory order so that T's debts were to be borne primarily by the residuary estate rather than by the £50 legacy.

Debts charged on the deceased's property: Where a person incurs a debt secured by a mortgage or charge on particular property owned by him, on his death that property continues to bear the primary liability for the repayment of the debt: s 35(1) AEA (see also *Re Turner* (1938)).

Section 35(1) is not applicable where property forming part of the deceased's estate is charged with a debt, but that debt did not come into being until after his death (see *Re Birmingham* (1959)).

Section 35(1) may also be displaced where a contrary intention appears in the deceased's will. This will be the case for instance where:

- A will directs that T's debts are to be paid out of his general estate or his residuary estate and in so doing refers to the charge. For example, 'I hereby direct that all my debts, including the mortgage debt charged on [description of property] are to be paid out of my residuary estate'.

Note, however, that if the material direction does not refer expressly or by implication to the charge, s 35(1) will remain in force.

- The will specifically directs that T's debts are to be paid out of a special fund, whether or not the direction refers to the charge expressly or by implication. If the fund is insufficient to repay the entire debt, however, the property on which the debt is charged remains primarily liable for the balance (see *Re Fegan* (1928) and *Re Birch* (1909)).

The position where two properties have been charged: Where two properties which were charged together are left to different persons, both properties will bear the burden of repaying the debt rateably (see *Re Neeld* (1962)).

By contrast, where two properties which were charged separately are left to the same beneficiary, neither property will bear the burden of the debt which was charged on the other property (see *Re Holt* (1916); *Frewen v Law Life Assurance Society* (1896) and *Re Baron Kensington* (1902)).

Marshalling: A creditor of the deceased is not bound by the statutory order of payment. However, if such a creditor obtains payment out of an asset which was not supposed to bear the burden of his debt, under the doctrine of *marshalling*, the beneficiary entitled to that asset may lay claim to the asset which should have borne the burden of the debt (see *Re Broadwood* (1911); *Re Cohen* (1960) and *Re Matthews' WT* (1961)).

Order of payment of debts where the estate is insolvent

An estate is insolvent if all the deceased's assets when realised are insufficient to meet all his expenses, debts and liabilities.

In such an event, the order in which the debts due to various creditors will be repaid out of the estate is as follows:

Debts of secured creditors: A secured creditor is entitled to obtain payment out of the property which serves as security for the debt, in priority to all other creditors. If the security is inadequate, he must then prove for the balance as an unsecured creditor.

Unsecured debts: A deceased's funeral, testamentary and administration expenses, provided they are reasonable, are accorded priority over the debts of unsecured creditors.

Such unsecured debts are payable in the following order:

- *Specially preferred debts*: eg money or property of a friendly society which was in the possession of the deceased as an officer of the society, even if he was no longer an officer at his death.
- *Preferential debts*: These include the following categories:
  - money owed to the Inland Revenue in respect of PAYE income tax deducted by the deceased from his employees;
  - VAT, car tax, betting and gaming duties;
  - social security contributions due from the deceased at his death;
  - any sums owed by the deceased in respect of contributions to occupational pension schemes and the state earnings related pension scheme;

- any amount owed by the deceased to an employee or ex-employee as remuneration or holiday pay.

- *Ordinary debts*: Most debts which fall outside the above categories are ordinary debts. As between themselves, ordinary debts rank equally and an ordinary creditor does not gain priority over other creditors by going to court and obtaining a judgment for his debt.

- *Interest* accruing on preferential and ordinary debts after the deceased's death.

- *Deferred debts*: These are in the nature of loans or other forms of credit given to the deceased by a person who was the spouse of the deceased at the time he or she died.

Distribution of the estate

Advertising for claims

After paying or providing for the payment of the deceased's debts and expenses, the prs can then distribute the deceased's estate. To facilitate distribution, s 27 TA empowers prs to advertise their intention to distribute and invite those interested in the estate to notify them within a specified time.

Once this is done, they may distribute without being liable to anyone who did not notify them of their claim (see *Re Aldhous* (1955)).

Another course open to a pr is to seek a *Benjamin order*. This is a court order empowering distribution of the deceased's estate on whatever footing the court directs. The name is derived from *Re Benjamin* (1902) where T in his will left a share of his residue to his son B. A year before T's death, B had disappeared without trace. The court ordered B's share to be distributed on the footing that he had died before T (see also *Re Taylor's Estate* (1969); *Re Lowe's WT* (1973) and *Re Green's WT* (1985)).

The position where a beneficiary owes money to the estate
Where a person entitled to a sum of money under a will or intestacy was indebted to the deceased, the prs may deduct the amount owed from what it pays that person (see, eg *Rhodesia Goldfield Ltd* (1910); *Re Akerman* (1891) and *Re Melton* (1918)).

It emerges from *Re Savage* (1918) that the prs can only adopt this course of action where the beneficiary affected is entitled to money and not some other species of property (eg colonial stock).

It has also been held in *Re Binns* (1929) that a pr cannot retain money due to a beneficiary in respect of a debt owed to the estate by some other person through whom the benefit was derived.

The position regarding infant beneficiaries
A trustee cannot ordinarily distribute property to infant beneficiaries since an infant cannot give a valid receipt for property or money to which he is entitled under a will or intestacy. *Note*, however, that:

- a married infant can give a valid receipt for income under s 21 LPA;
- a will may expressly direct that the entitlement of an infant beneficiary is to be paid to him during infancy and that a receipt given by the infant will be valid; although it is more common for property to be held on trust for infant beneficiaries either under the terms of the will or under s 42 AEA 1925.

Appropriation

Under s 41 AEA, the prs may appropriate any part of the deceased's estate in or towards satisfying any legacy, interest or share in the deceased's estate.

For purposes of appropriation an asset is to be valued as at the date of the appropriation (see *Re Chateris* (1917) and *Re Collins* (1975)).

Rights of beneficiaries pending distribution

Before distribution of the deceased's estate, ownership of his assets vests in his prs. They do not hold the estate as trustees in the strict sense and a beneficiary acquires no equitable interest in the estate at that point. All he has is a right to ensure that the estate is properly administered (see *Commissioner of Stamp Duties (Queensland) v Livingstone* (1965) and *Re Leigh's WT* (1970)).

Assents

An assent is an indication by a pr that he does not require a particular asset for purposes of administration and that it can pass to the beneficiary entitled to it.

- *Personalty*: At common law, assents could be given only in respect of personalty and leaseholds. Such assents require no strict formalities and may be written, oral or implied from conduct as was the case in *Solomon v Attenborough* (1913).
- *Land*: Under s 36 AEA, a pr may assent to the vesting of any estate or interest in real property owned by the deceased. The assent may be made in favour of a beneficiary or his trustee.

Section 36 does not apply to any real property of the deceased which did not devolve on the pr when the deceased died but came into his hands by other means. In effect, the vesting of such property on the person entitled to it must be by means of a conveyance and not an assent (see *Re Stirrup's Contract* (1961)).

Where equitable interests in land are concerned, an assent may be verbal or by conduct (see *Re Edwards' WT* (1982)). However, where a legal estate is involved, it must be in writing and signed by the pr.

If a testator devises property to his executor, beneficially or as a trustee, it has been held in *Re King's WT* (1964) that the executor must assent in writing in order for the legal estate to vest in him as a beneficiary or trustee.

The position of personal representatives who are also trustees

It is not uncommon for the same person to be a pr and a trustee in respect of the same estate of the deceased. In such a case, it may have to be decided whether he is acting as a pr or a trustee at any particular point in time since the two offices differ in several respects, most notably:

- Executors exercise their authority jointly and severally, but trustees must act jointly (see *Solomon v Attenborough*).
- A sole pr can issue a valid receipt to a purchaser of land but a sole trustee (other than a trust corporation) cannot.
- A trustee's paramount duty is to balance the interests of the beneficiaries to whom the property belongs. However, a pr's duty is to consider the interest of the deceased's estate as a whole rather than seek to balance the interests of various beneficiaries (see *Re Hayes' WT* (1971)).

- Where a sole pr dies without fully administering the estate and there is no executorship by representation, a *grant of administration de bonis non* will be made. By contrast if a sole trustee dies, the trust estate will devolve on his own pr.
- Different limitation periods apply to actions brought against a trustee and against a pr.